MENSA

PRESENTS

THE ULTIMATE PUZZLE CHALLENGE

THIS IS A CARLTON BOOK

Text and puzzle content copyright © British
Mensa Limited 1999
Design and artwork copyright © Carlton
Books Limited 1999

This edition published by Carlton Books
Limited 1999

A CIP Catalogue for this book is available
from the British Library

ISBN 1 85868 716 0

Executive Editor: Tim Dedopulos
Design: Paul Messam
Production: Alexia Turner

Printed and bound in England

MENSA

PRESENTS

THE ULTIMATE PUZZLE CHALLENGE

JOHN BREMNER,
PHILIP CARTER AND KEN RUSSELL

CARLTON

British Mensa Ltd

British Mensa Ltd is an organization for individuals who have one common trait: an IQ in the top 2% of the nation. Over 40,000 current members have found out how bright they are. This leaves room for an additional 1.5 million members in Britain alone. You may be one of them.

Looking for intellectual stimulation?

If you enjoy mental exercise, you'll find lots of good "workout programs" in our national monthly magazine. Voice your opinion in one of the newsletters published by our many local chapters. Learn from the many books and publications that are available to you as a member.

Looking for social interaction?

Are you a "people person," or would you like to meet other people with whom you feel comfortable? Then come to our local meetings, parties, and get-togethers. Participate in our lectures and debates. Attend our regional events and national gatherings. There's something happening on the Mensa calendar almost daily. So, you have lots of opportunities to meet people, exchange ideas, and make interesting new friends.

Looking for others who share your special interest?

Whether yours is as common as crossword puzzles or as esoteric as Egyptology, there's a Mensa Special Interest Group (SIG) for it.

Take the challenge. Find out how smart you really are. Contact British Mensa Ltd today and ask for a free brochure. We enjoy adding new members and ideas to our high-IQ organization.

British Mensa Ltd
Mensa House
St. John's Square
Wolverhampton
WV2 4AH

Or, if you don't live in Great Britain and you'd like more details, you can contact:

Mensa International
15 The Ivories
628 Northampton Street
London N1 2NY
England

who will be happy to put you in touch with your own national Mensa.

Contents

PUZZLE 1

Here is an easy one to start you off. Which of these patterns fits into the blank section?

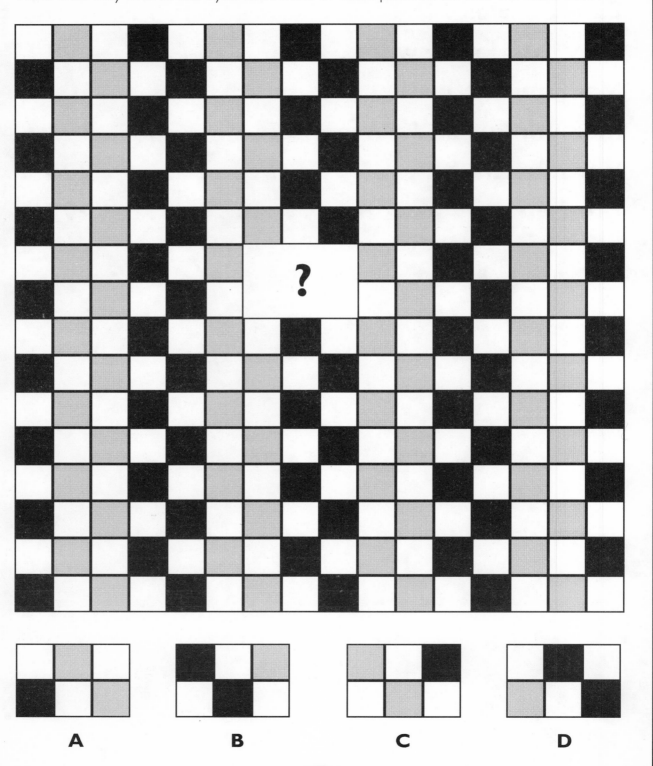

A   **B**   **C**   **D**

PUZZLE 2

Can you find the missing number in D ?

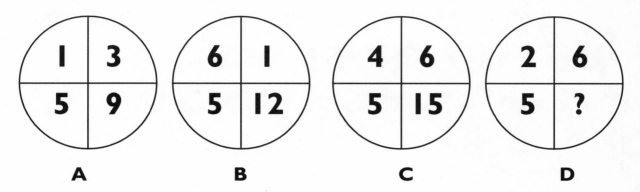

A   B   C   D

PUZZLE 3

Which of the symbols in the box (A, B, or C), should replace the question mark ?

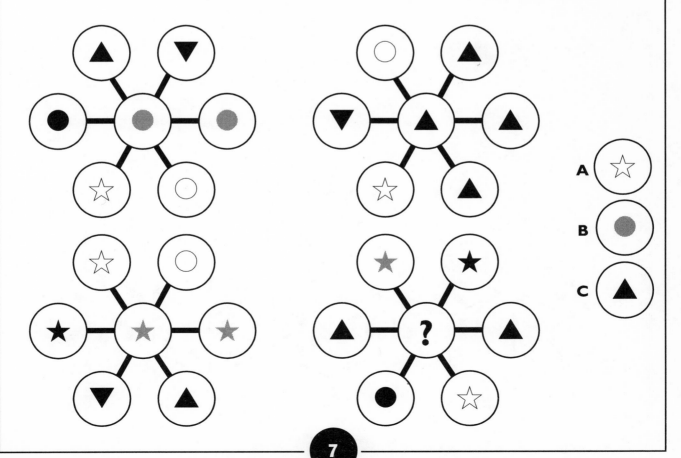

LEVEL 1

PUZZLE 4

What has three hands, but no feet?

PUZZLE 5

Continue this sequence.

t w t f s ?

PUZZLE 6

Which is the only cube that can be made from this layout ?

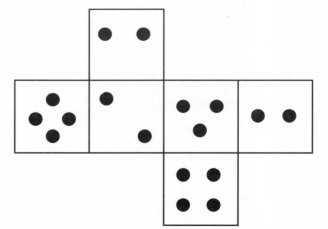

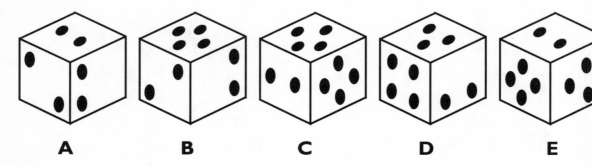

A   B   C   D   E

PUZZLE 7

Here's a trick one.

How many months have 30 days?

PUZZLE 8

Can you find the missing number in this segmented circle ?

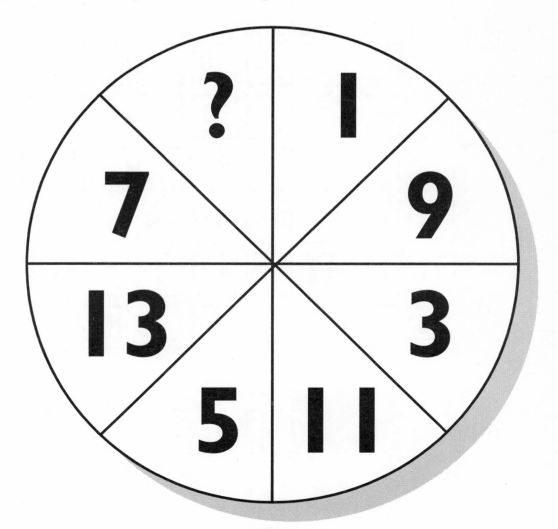

PUZZLE 9

Can you re-assemble these blocks of three into the blanks to form a magic square in which the numbers in each row, column and long diagonal add to 175 ?

27

6 8 17

30 39 48

35

1 10 19

36

31 40 49

45

4

38

18

12

46

26

5

34

13 15 24 33 42 44

21 23 32 41 43 3

22

28

29

14 16 25

37

2 11 20

47 7 9

PUZZLE 10

Can you solve the following anagrams to find the names of eight countries?

> **VISUAL YOGA**
> **AS A RITUAL**
> **COLD ANTS**
> **SIR USA**
> **OUR HANDS**
> **A FRUIT CHAOS**
> **GREY MAN**
> **BAD BOARS**

PUZZLE 11

This diagram was constructed according to a certain logic. Can you decipher the logic and find the missing number?

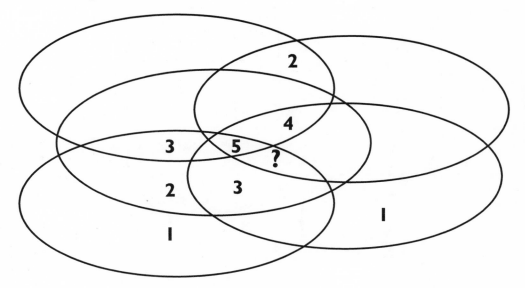

PUZZLE 12

Can you figure out what number should replace the question mark ?

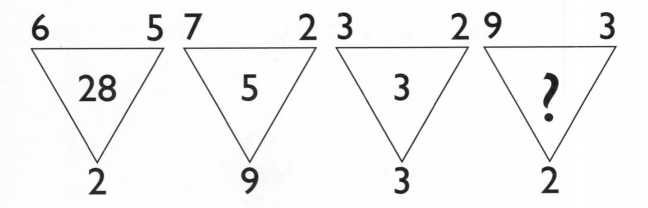

PUZZLE 13

What is significant about this nonsense sentence ?

RED   ZAW
THIS
JOUNG   CYMLK
PBQ   XFV

PUZZLE 14

How can you change these ten lines into nine lines, without drawing an attachment between any of them, or adding any new lines, or covering a line, or rubbing any of the lines out?

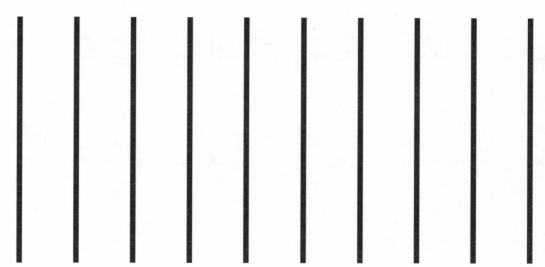

PUZZLE 15

Can you draw the hands in the correct position on the blank clock face ?

PUZZLE 16

Can you figure out what comes next ?

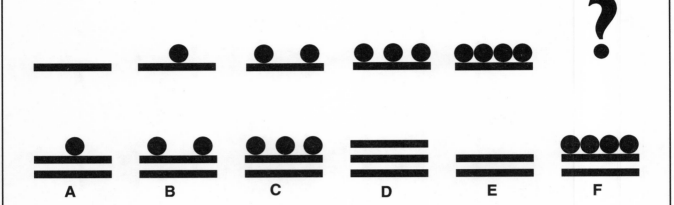

PUZZLE 17

Why is the number TEN afraid of the number SEVEN?

PUZZLE 18

Can you find the single symbol, A, B, or C, that will balance the bottom set of scales?

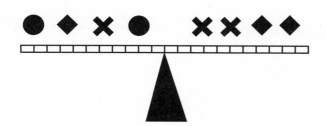

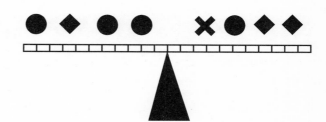

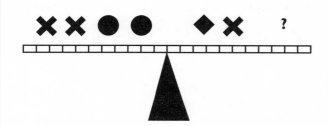

A   B   c

PUZZLE 19

Can you find the odd-ball out?

313

119

511

016

214

115

412

PUZZLE 20

In this diagram, starting from the top of the diamond and working in a clockwise direction, the three basic mathematical symbols +, ×, -, have been omitted. Your task is to restore them so that the solution in the middle is correct.

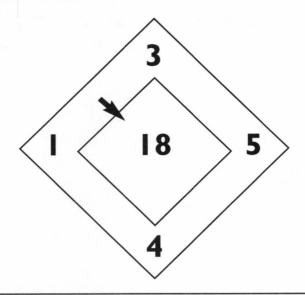

PUZZLE 21

Can you solve the following anagrams of famous rock/pop groups names?

THE ABLE SET
STRONGEST IN HELLO
I SKETCHED MAN
MACHINE
A COMET FLOWED
FONDLY KIP
IT IS RED STAR

PUZZLE 22

The dial represents an old fashioned telephone dial, with letters and numbers. Beside it is a list of numbers representing ten cities of the world. Can you use the dial to decode them ?

A   61637

B   437155

C   455255

D   5290564

E   732520

F   6552

G   5167234427

H   53415

I   75405

J   173257

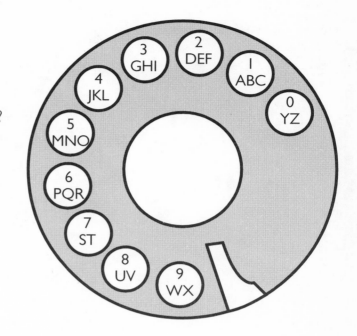

PUZZLE 23

Can you find the odd-clown-out?

A   B   C

D   E   F

PUZZLE 24

Can you complete the analogy?

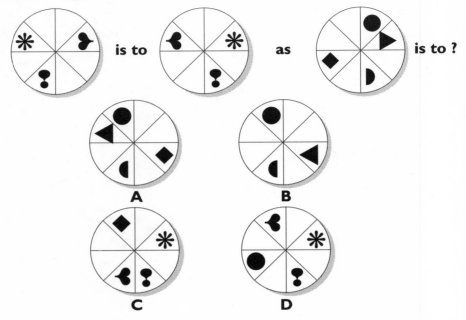

PUZZLE 25

Which character should be next in the sequence in the sequence after F ?
Should it be G, H, or I ?

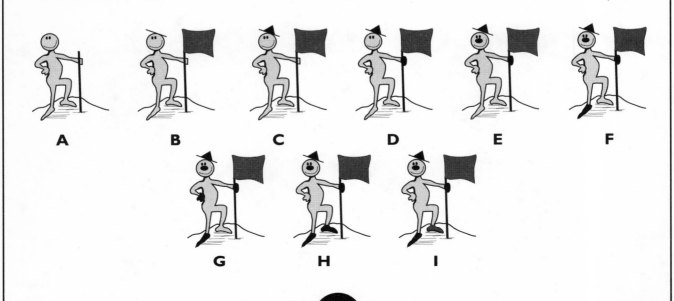

PUZZLE 26

Why is a 'policy cash log' mental?

PUZZLE 27

In each row of the grid below, the name of an American city is concealed. Use the key provided to decode the cities. There is an added complication in that the letter A can be represented by either 1, or 9, or both.

1	2	3	4	5	6	7	8	9
a	b	c	d	e	f	g	h	i
j	k	l	m	n	o	p	q	r
s	t	u	v	w	x	y	z	a

A | 7 | 2 | 2 | 3 | 8 | 9 | 3 | 1 | 7 | 6 | 4 | 3 | 1 | 1 | 9 | 8

B | 6 | 1 | 5 | 1 | 9 | 9 | 3 | 8 | 5 | 7 | 5 | 5 | 5 | 5 | 6 | 9

C | 2 | 4 | 9 | 4 | 9 | 1 | 6 | 5 | 8 | 4 | 3 | 4 | 5 | 3 | 8 | 2

D | 3 | 7 | 7 | 3 | 5 | 1 | 1 | 8 | 4 | 9 | 3 | 3 | 5 | 9 | 1 | 1

E | 1 | 3 | 7 | 5 | 2 | 4 | 2 | 4 | 9 | 1 | 2 | 6 | 9 | 1 | 5 | 5

F | 4 | 4 | 9 | 9 | 4 | 9 | 4 | 7 | 6 | 5 | 7 | 5 | 3 | 9 | 9 | 1

PUZZLE 28

Can you place these sets of twin blocks back into the diagram in such a way that all rows, columns, and long diagonals add to 65 ?

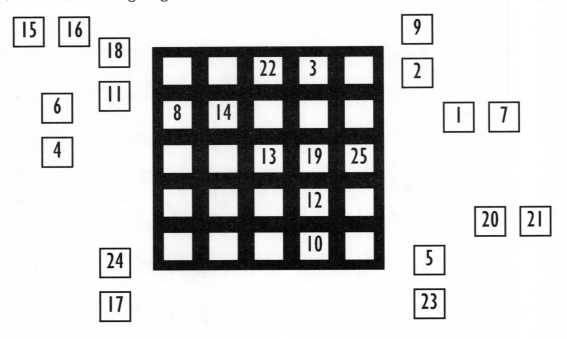

PUZZLE 29

Can you solve these anagrams to find eight basic elements. Oxygen, for example, is an element.

DOG HENRY   RING TONE

PUSH OR SHOP   LICE HORN

TAUT MINI   ACNE SIR

NAME AGNES   AMUSING ME

PUZZLE 30

The black spots on this grid have been placed according to a very exact logic. One black spot has been left out. Can you figure out the correct position where it should go ?

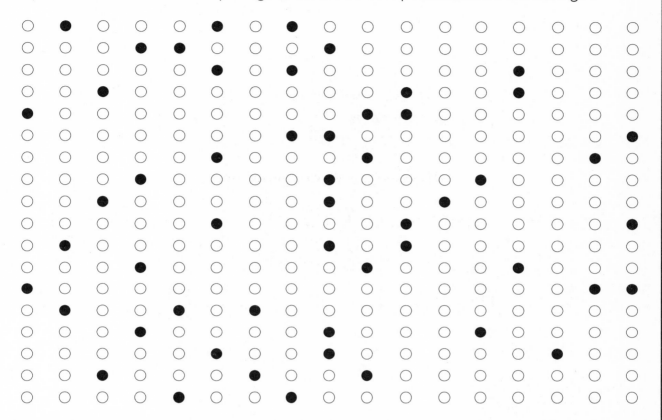

PUZZLE 31

You are a detective who has to solve a terrible mystery.......

On a still calm day in the middle of a still calm week, in the middle of summer, an unanchored yacht was found two hundred miles off-shore, surrounded by six people who had all drowned.
They were all wearing swimming costumes, were known to have been recreational swimmers, and (apart from having drowned) were otherwise unharmed.

Why did they drown ?

PUZZLE 32

This is a two part puzzle.

a. Can you find the following words in the grid below ? :

BELLS; FISHES; BEES; SLEEP; BIRDS; BONES; DREAMS; EGGS; FIRE.

b. Can you link each of the words you find with its appropriate `ology' from the following list ?

OSTEOLOGY; HYPNOLOGY; CAMPANOLOGY; ICHTHYOLOGY; PYROLOGY; APIOLOGY; ORNITHOLOGY; OOLOGY; ONEIRILOGY.

Words may appear written in any direction.

Z	R	O	N	M	P	D	R	E	A	M	S	O	O	L	K	I
P	G	J	K	V	J	K	N	L	K	Z	H	G	H	J	K	O
A	L	R	B	O	C	J	I	O	P	R	A	B	L	A	I	M
T	R	I	D	E	W	A	S	T	A	B	L	A	N	R	I	N
N	O	N	S	E	L	N	N	S	E	W	U	R	D	Z	A	E
I	M	P	E	L	S	L	P	E	O	P	B	C	R	T	R	R
T	R	A	K	B	E	M	S	E	K	A	I	M	E	M	T	I
C	L	E	S	T	F	R	O	F	A	C	R	P	R	P	C	F
A	N	E	R	I	S	E	N	U	D	O	D	O	M	I	C	L
Q	U	E	S	V	O	V	A	I	M	N	S	T	H	I	B	R
E	G	H	A	M	C	P	L	U	N	D	T	O	O	B	Y	N
R	E	I	L	L	I	N	E	R	G	A	N	D	O	Y	P	O
S	L	H	I	V	E	R	S	E	O	F	G	N	U	N	G	E
E	L	U	O	E	T	T	S	O	L	O	E	E	O	F	A	L
A	H	P	N	E	N	O	O	P	E	S	T	L	H	E	P	O
K	H	G	A	B	T	V	H	L	E	G	G	O	A	M	V	E
S	T	R	E	G	G	S	O	O	M	W	A	N	N	T	I	R

PUZZLE 33

Can you use the logic behind A & B to complete C?

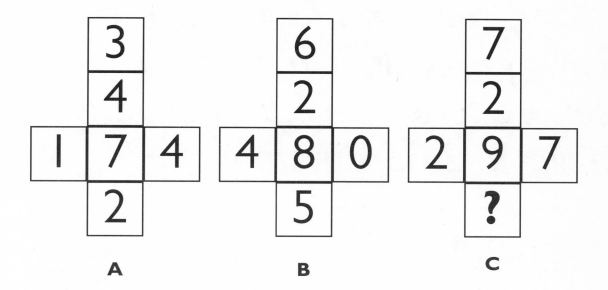

A   B   C

PUZZLE 34

Can you find the letter of the alphabet that should replace the question mark?

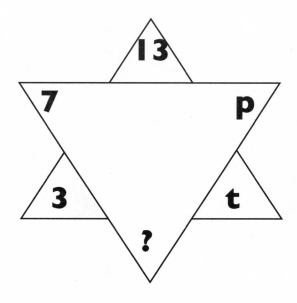

PUZZLE 35

A dog can run fifty miles in a day. How far could it run into a square forest of 2500 square miles in 2.05 days?

PUZZLE 36

Can you pick the odd-one-out from this set?

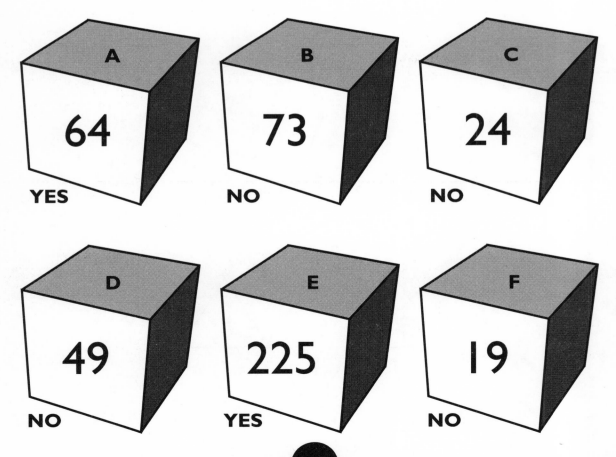

A
64
YES

B
73
NO

C
24
NO

D
49
NO

E
225
YES

F
19
NO

PUZZLE 37

Can you use the table to find the missing letter to replace the question mark in C ?

a	b	c
d	e	f
g	h	i
j	k	l
m	n	o
p	q	r
s	t	u
v	w	x
y	z	a

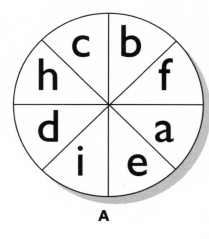

A

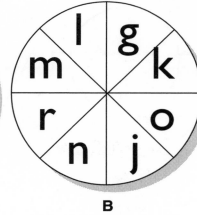

B

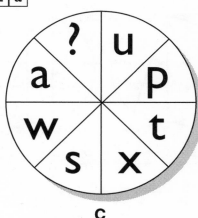

C

PUZZLE 38

One of these squares is different from the others in a particular way. Can you find the odd-one-out?

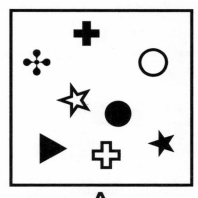

A

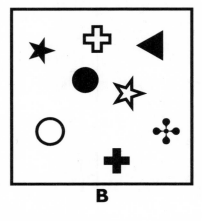

B

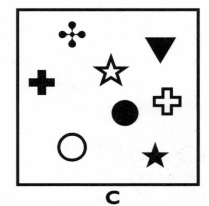

C

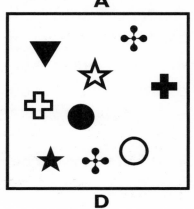

D

PUZZLE 39

Can you find which of these sets does not go with the other three ?

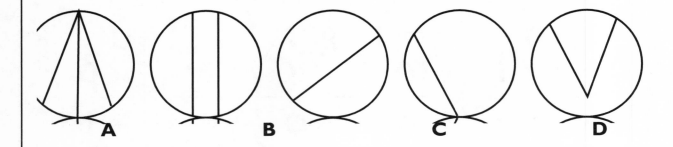

A   B   C   D

PUZZLE 40

You've been given the chance to join the boardroom of a company which has a strange rule. Before you get to join, two papers — one with "yes" written on it and one with "no" written on it — are folded up and placed in a box. You must pick out one of the papers (without looking), and if you choose the one with "yes" written on it, you become a director. Otherwise, you are sacked on the spot and thrown out of the building.

On this occasion, a mean-spirited ex-partner of yours has substituted for the paper with "yes" written on it, another one with "no" written on it. Just before you go in, he gleefully informs you of what he has done and that you are doomed to be sacked. You are not permitted to speak during the ceremony, nor will you have a chance to switch the papers in the box your-self in time.

How will you avoid being sacked ?

PUZZLE 41

The dial represents an old fashioned telephone dial, with letters and numbers. Beside it is a list of numbers representing ten famous composers. Can you use the dial to decode their names ?

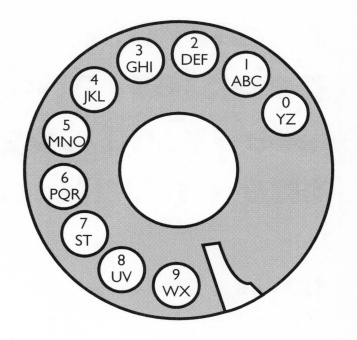

A   1113
B   31025
C   550167
D   913526
E   513426
F   71381267
G   7761835743
H   757115353
I   16814526
J   71313458743

PUZZLE 42

Can you figure out what number should go in the middle of C ?

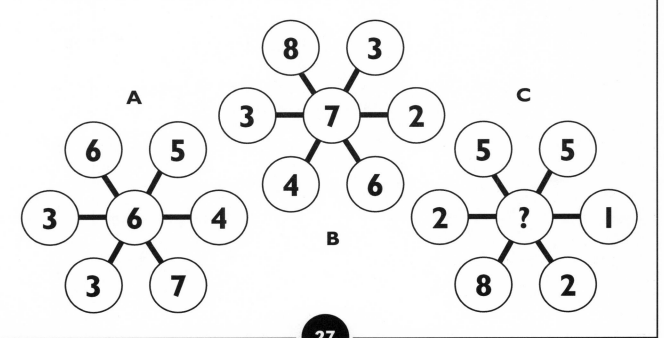

PUZZLE 43

A carrot, a pile of pebbles, and a pipe are lying together in the middle of a field.

Why ?

PUZZLE 44

Can you find the logic in these clocks and draw the hands on the blank clock.

PUZZLE 45

The names of seven Presidents of the USA are hidden in these anagrams. Can you find them ?

**sweet groaning hog
I relax in much dishonor
likely lawn mimic
lost hero or devotee
good in vice call
harsh nuclear treat
no jobless on hand in NY**

PUZZLE 46

Using only the numbers that have already been used here, can you fill the blanks of this square to make every column, row, and long diagonal total 24 ?

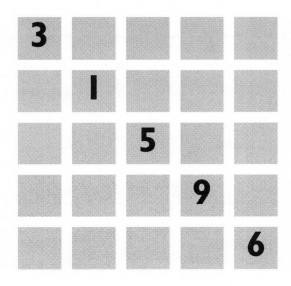

PUZZLE 47

Rearrange the lines of this puzzle to find a famous quotation by Thomas Paine about the sublime and the ridiculous.

O	N	E		S	T	E	P		A	B	O	V	E		T	H
O	F	T	E	N		S	O		N	E	A	R	L	Y		R
H	E		R	I	D	I	C	U	L	O	U	S		A	N	D
S		T	H	E	M		S	E	P	A	R	A	T	E	L	Y
E	L	A	T	E	D		T	H	A	T		I	T		I	S
D	I	F	F	I	C	U	L	T		T	O		C	L	A	S
T	H	E		S	U	B	L	I	M	E		A	N	D		T
E		S	U	B	L	I	M	E		M	A	K	E	S		T
E		R	I	D	I	C	U	L	O	U	S		M	A	K	E
H	E		R	I	D	I	C	U	L	O	U	S		A	R	E
S		T	H	E		S	U	B	L	I	M	E		A	G	A
O	N	E		S	T	E	P		A	B	O	V	E		T	H
I	N	-	T	H	O	M	A	S		P	A	I	N	E		

I	N	-	T	H	O	M	A	S		P	A	I	N	E		

PUZZLE 48

Which is the only cube shown here that can be made from this layout?

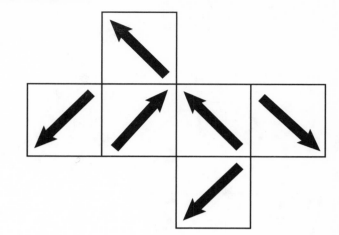

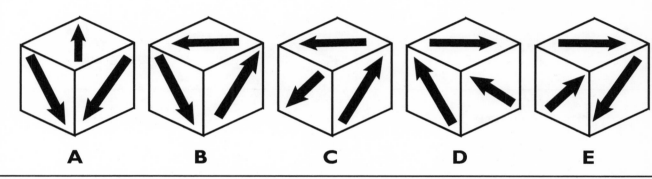

A   B   C   D   E

PUZZLE 49

As an entrance test for a university you are given a corked bottle with a coin in it. Your task is to remove the coin without taking the cork out of the bottle or breaking the glass, or boring a hole in the cork or glass.

How do you pass the test and get the coin out?

PUZZLE 50

Can you find the missing number that should replace the question mark in the last wheel ?

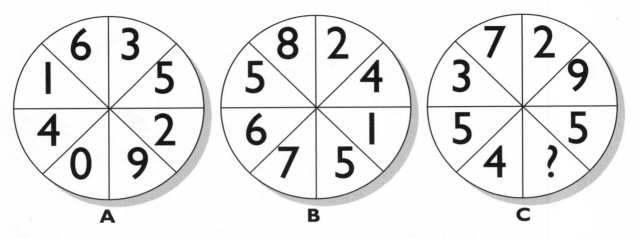

A   B   C

PUZZLE 51

Can you work out which tile fits into the blank section of this pattern?

A

B

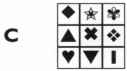

C

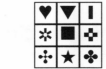

D

PUZZLE 52

**I live at the beginning of eternity;
At the end of time and space;
I am the beginning of every end,
And the end of every place.
*Who am I ?***

PUZZLE 53

This Roman numeral equation is wrong. Can you make it work by moving just one line?

XIIV + XVII = XXX

PUZZLE 54

Can you work out the missing value in this set of barcodes ?

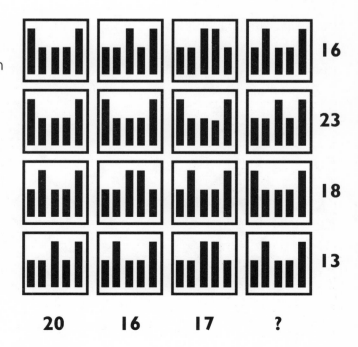

PUZZLE 55

Can you work out how many hexagons like the one on the right are in this collection ?

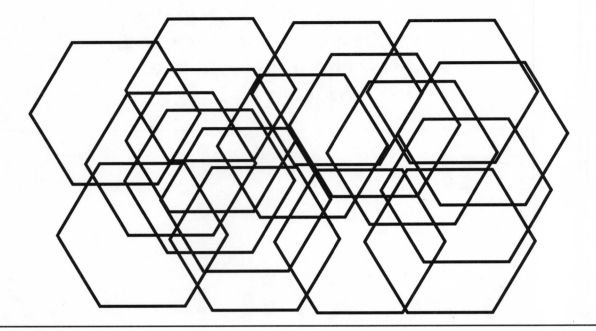

PUZZLE 56

In this diagram, starting from the top of the diamond and working in a clockwise direction applying the operands shown, each symbol stands for a number, with the same symbol always being the same number. Taking each calculation in turn, can you work out the value that should be in the middle of C ?

A   B   C

PUZZLE 57

Can you decipher this famous quotation by J. Abbot? To make it slightly more difficult, the spacings of the words have been removed, although the anagram of each word is in the correct sequential place in the sentence. The line endings shown here may not coincide with word endings.

> *Ahdlicacnsakadt*
> *ushaonsnueosqit*
> *ttahtehtswiesn*
> *matoncnasarewn.*

PUZZLE 58

Can you figure out what number comes next in this sequence?

143, 120, 99, 80, 63, 48, ...

PUZZLE 59

Can you find the following tools and equipment in the puzzle below?

HAMMER, PUNCH, BRADAWL, TOOLBELT, PLIERS, HANDPLANE, FILE, CHISEL, SCREWDRIVER, SAW, NAILS, SPANNER, PINCERS, COUNTERSINKER, DRILL, RIVETS, MACHINERY, KNIVES, RATCHET, SAFETY HELMET, TILES.

S	L	L	P	U	N	C	H	I	T	B	I	O	B	T	I	H
R	X	V	H	J	T	E	M	L	E	H	Y	T	E	F	A	S
L	T	B	R	A	D	A	W	L	N	T	A	I	T	M	O	T
L	Y	A	A	S	O	R	R	R	C	K	L	L	M	E	I	B
J	U	O	T	O	O	L	B	E	L	T	D	E	A	B	A	W
P	B	A	C	I	S	T	A	I	P	S	R	S	C	E	M	I
L	N	O	H	O	A	K	B	T	I	E	I	N	H	O	Q	T
I	M	E	E	I	W	N	U	E	N	R	L	T	I	W	E	R
E	I	S	T	A	B	I	A	V	C	E	L	O	N	P	N	W
R	U	L	I	O	I	V	O	W	E	L	W	T	E	L	A	I
S	Y	I	S	C	R	E	W	D	R	I	V	E	R	E	L	T
L	K	A	T	B	E	S	T	R	S	F	T	O	Y	S	P	D
N	O	N	I	Y	T	E	O	I	T	O	A	E	E	I	D	T
B	O	L	P	E	X	E	A	W	E	B	T	I	E	H	N	E
Y	I	L	V	R	E	N	N	A	P	S	A	B	Z	C	A	I
B	S	I	E	T	W	O	T	Z	P	T	O	E	W	P	H	W
A	R	E	K	N	I	S	R	E	T	N	U	O	C	A	O	T
S	D	F	X	I	E	A	E	W	A	I	E	O	I	P	Z	B

PUZZLE 60

Which is the odd one out?

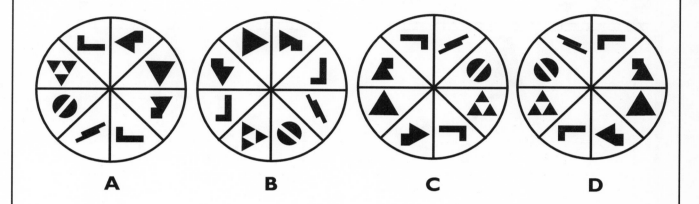

A   B   C   D

PUZZLE 61

Can you work out what number should go into the last square ?

8   3   1   13   4   9

2   4   8   2   5   6

PUZZLE 62

Can you work out how many crosses are required to balance the lower scales ?

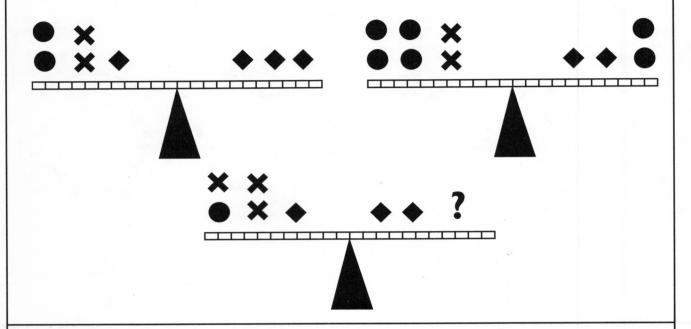

PUZZLE 63

Marianne lived alone in a big house. She rarely left her house and spent most of her time maintaining the property, reading classical literature, and listening to music. One evening she ran out of food and decided to go to the 24 hour shop for some more. Upon leaving, she turned off the TV & lights. She was away for a couple of hours, but to her horror, when she got back she found that she was responsible for the deaths of eighty people.

What happened to them ?

PUZZLE 64

Can you re-assemble these blocks of three into the blanks to form a magic square in which the numbers in each row, column and long diagonal add to 196 ?

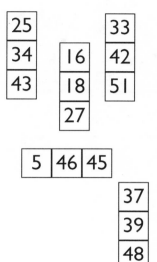

Blocks and grid:

- 25 / 34 / 43
- 16 / 18 / 27
- 33 / 42 / 51
- 8 49 41
- 9 / 11 / 20
- 5 46 45
- 37 / 39 / 48
- 13 / 22 / 31
- 21 / 30 / 32
- 23 15 7

Main grid:

24						
26		17		50		
35		19		10		
52	44	36	28		12	4
				29		
14	6	47		38		
				40		

PUZZLE 65

Here are the anagrams of seven famous writers, none of whom are still living. Can you discover their identities? The words formed by the anagrams are not clues.

A SLIM HELP AWAKES IRE

HOLY SMART ALEC

HOLES JAM NOUNS

CARRY HUGE COFFEE

POOCH ENDS RAJ

SKIN HELD SCARCE

I'M A CHEMICALLY WEAK PARAKEET

PUZZLE 66

Can you work out which of the below triangles (A, B, C, or D) is the solution to this analogy?

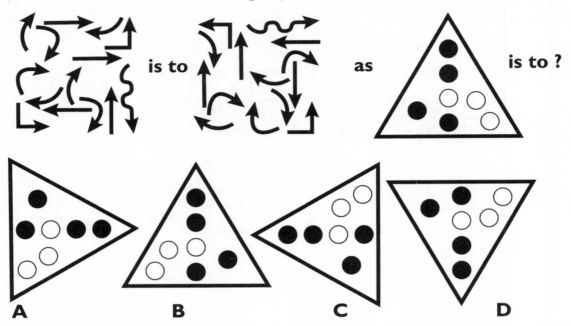

A   **B**   **C**   **D**

PUZZLE 67

Can you figure out the next two numbers in this extended sequence ?
The sequence is not as random as it seems.

8, 5, 3, 8, 1, 9, 0, 9, 9, 8, 7, 5,
2, 7, 9, 6, 5, 1, 6, 7, 3, 0, 3, 3,
6, 9, 5, 4, 9, 3, 2, 5, 7, 2, 9, 1,
0, 1, 1, 2, 3, 5, 8, 3, 1, 4, 5, 9,
4, 3, 7, 0, 7, 7, 4, ... , ...

PUZZLE 68

How can you prove that a man has three heads?

PUZZLE 69

Can you find the odd-one-out between these five cubes ?

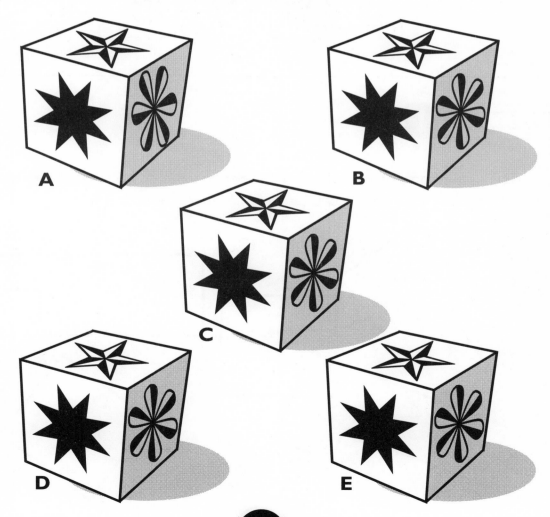

PUZZLE 70

Can you work out the value of the symbols, and hence the missing value ?

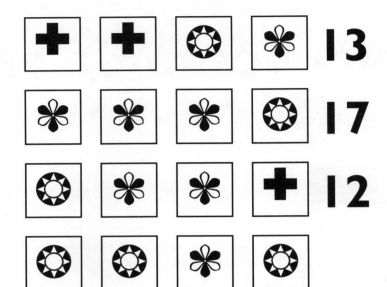

PUZZLE 71

Jane came home from school and found that her sister, Voilet, had cut up her favourite film poster into the following shapes. Can you help her fit it back together ?

PUZZLE 72

Somewhere within this grid is a 4 x 4 block in which every row, column, and long diagonal adds to 34. Can you find it ?

16	3	2	13	15	10	3	6	41	15	14	4	12	8	7	1	12
5	10	11	8	4	5	16	9	9	7	6	12	5	11	10	8	5
9	6	7	12	14	11	2	13	16	3	2	13	15	10	3	6	5
41	15	14	4	12	8	7	1	5	10	11	8	4	5	16	9	15
16	3	2	13	15	10	3	6	15	10	16	2	3	13	16	2	3
5	10	11	8	4	5	16	9	4	5	5	11	10	8	5	11	10
9	6	7	12	14	11	2	13	14	11	9	7	6	12	9	7	6
41	15	14	4	12	8	7	1	12	8	4	14	15	1	14	15	1
9	7	6	12	5	11	10	8	5	11	10	3	6	41	15	14	4
4	14	15	1	9	7	6	12	9	7	5	16	9	9	7	6	12
12	8	13	13	4	14	15	1	4	14	11	2	13	16	3	2	13

PUZZLE 73

This diagram was constructed to a certain logic. Can you work out which letter should replace the question mark ?

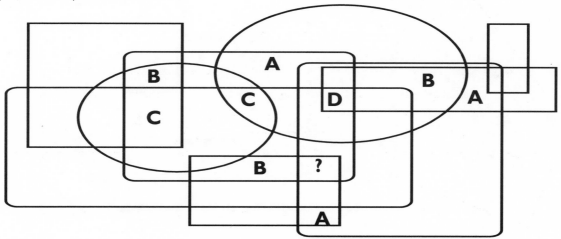

PUZZLE 74

Can you decipher the following transport code to find a famous quote by H.W. Longfellow? Words are separated by spaces. (Eg: There are three words in the 1st line.) Each symbol always stands for the same letter. The end of each line is the end of a word, and the following words are part of the sentence, but in a mixed up order.

do explain time thing it takes right you why less

PUZZLE 75

One of these split balls does not go with the others. Can you pick it out?

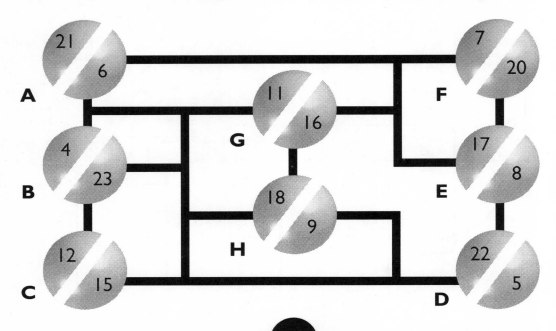

PUZZLE 76

On a pool table are 12 balls of identical size. All are the same weight except one, which is slightly heavier than each of the others, but not enough for you to be able to tell just by holding it.

The person you love has brought a set of balance scales, and has promised to be yours if you can tell which ball is heavier with just three weighings on the scales. Otherwise, you will be on your own for ever. Can you pass the test ?

PUZZLE 77

In this grid, the eighteen items of clothing may go up, down, along, backwards or forwards, but they all have a bend somewhere:

See if you can find the following words.
TIGHTS,
HANDKERCHIEF,
TROUSERS,
SKIRT,
DRESS,
STOCKINGS,
WAISTCOAT,
KNICKERS,
SHOES,
TIE,
PULLOVER,
UNDERWEAR,
HAT,
SHIRT, BLOUSE,
BRASSIERE,
SOCKS,
SUSPENDERS.

T	P	K	A	C	K	D	N	A	H	C	T	H	G	I	T	A
R	Q	T	R	T	E	I	R	B	C	E	S	E	R	E	D	C
O	C	Z	I	B	R	A	T	W	E	S	Q	A	Z	B	R	E
U	L	B	K	N	C	W	S	E	O	H	N	L	O	V	E	R
S	E	R	S	P	H	O	R	A	R	E	A	L	R	O	S	S
X	T	R	E	B	I	S	Q	K	O	I	Z	U	R	A	K	B
C	O	T	S	Z	E	H	W	V	C	T	L	P	A	U	Z	R
K	L	A	W	E	F	I	R	T	A	O	B	M	E	T	L	A
I	W	A	I	X	N	K	Q	O	H	I	N	K	W	N	B	E
N	E	N	S	E	R	S	E	M	A	T	R	X	R	I	X	R
G	W	C	T	U	E	C	S	X	R	N	E	V	E	D	N	U
S	T	A	C	Q	K	Z	U	B	A	I	R	O	K	Y	B	W
U	B	E	O	B	N	X	O	L	B	L	E	T	N	R	O	A
R	K	O	A	N	I	K	W	U	K	T	I	O	A	Z	L	K
Y	I	E	T	U	C	O	B	R	A	S	S	W	I	B	V	E
Z	S	N	M	X	K	N	E	R	Q	U	E	C	K	S	T	R
O	R	B	S	R	E	V	T	B	U	R	X	O	I	E	N	Q
R	E	D	N	E	P	S	U	S	A	T	E	S	T	A	X	B

PUZZLE 78

What question can you never answer "yes" to ?

PUZZLE 79

Can you work out the last digit in this sequence ?

1651, 2533, 3442, 4540, 5305, 6124,

7240, 8131, 9310, 10921, 11542, 12361,

13900, 14503, 15052, 16114, 1710 ....

PUZZLE 80

One of this pair of drama masks are not true mirror-images. Can you discover which pair ?

PUZZLE 81

The dial represents an old fashioned telephone dial, with letters and numbers. Beside it is a list of numbers representing ten adjective words. Adjectives are words that describe a noun.

For example: It was a very 'confusing' book. Book is the noun. Confusing is the adjective.

Can you use the dial to decode the adjectives?

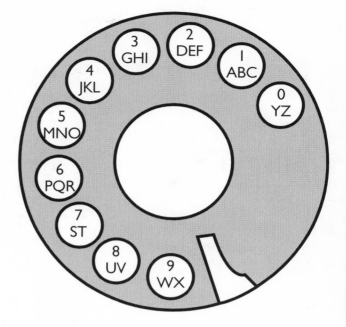

A	21713517353	**D**	16100	**G**	722817382	**J**	2513157353
B	5876132587	**E**	166214353	**H**	8316157		
C	14486353	**F**	76877956730	**I**	224313587		

PUZZLE 82

Two of these squares are in the wrong place in the sequence. Can you spot which two?

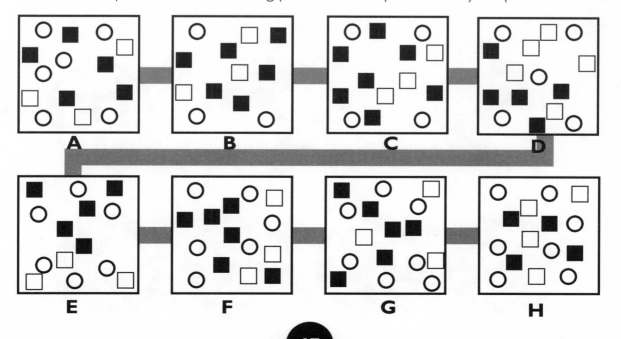

A   B   C   D

E   F   G   H

PUZZLE 83

What number is odd because it is even?

PUZZLE 84

Can you work out the value of the symbols, and hence the missing value ?

    11

    15

    13

PUZZLE 85

Can you work out the solution to this analogy ?

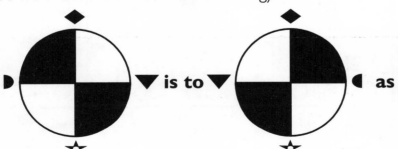 is to ▼ as  is to ?

A   B   C   D

48

PUZZLE 86

Can you figure out how to assemble these shapes to make a rectangle ?

PUZZLE 87

Can you put these columns and the 7 individual numbers into the proper place in the grid so that every row, column, and long diagonal add to 154 ?

34	1	9				42				17	25	26
32	41	0				33				8	16	24
23	39	40				31				-1	7	15
14	30	38				22				46	-2	6
5	21	29				13				37	45	4
3	12	20				11				28	36	44
43	10	18				2				19	27	35

PUZZLE 88

Can you solve the following anagrams to find ten vegetables ?

COOL CRIB

AWFUL RECOIL

CULT TEE

VEINED

PASTE TOO

SORT CAR

HIPS CAN

CRY EEL

SNOG IN PRISON

REACH IT OK

A SUGAR SAP

BOSS SPURS RESULT

PUZZLE 89

This Roman equation is wrong. Can you remove one Roman numeral to make it work?

XXiX + XXVi =

PUZZLE 90

Can you find the missing number ?

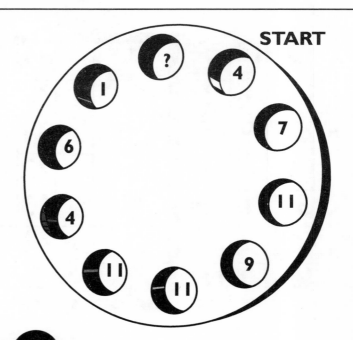

START

LEVEL 1

PUZZLE 91

Can you work out which tile fits into the blank section of this panel ?

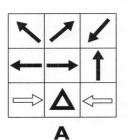

A

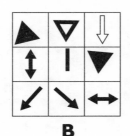

B

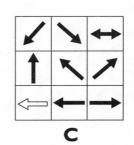

C

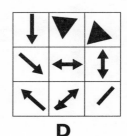

D

51

PUZZLE 92

Can you figure out what number should go in the middle of C ?

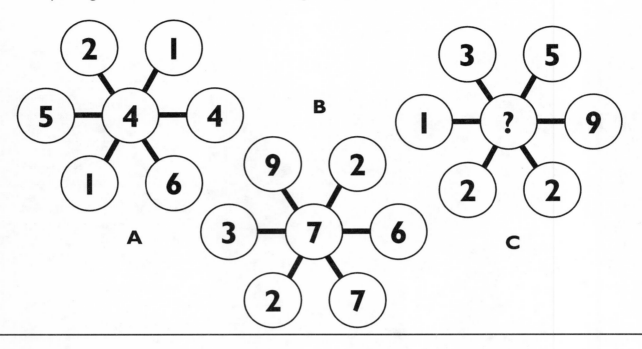

PUZZLE 93

Can you decipher this famous quotation by Walt Disney ? To make it slightly more difficult, the spacings of the words have been removed, although the anagram of each word is in the correct sequential place in the sentence. The line endings shown here may not coincide with word endings.

Lalruomdesarac nmoecuterfiewa hevehtegcuaoro tuuerpsmhet.

PUZZLE 94

Can you work out what number should go in the last square.

  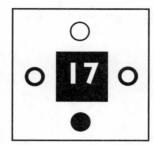 

PUZZLE 95

This diagram was constructed to a certain logic. Can you work out what number/s should replace A & B in this diagram ?

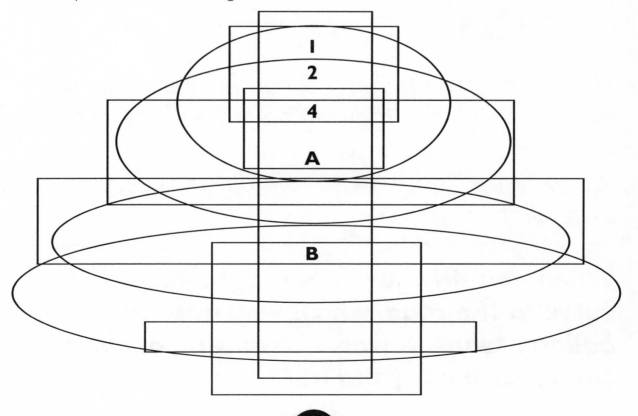

PUZZLE 96

Can you find the last two digits of this sequence ?

97, 142, 209, 306, 448, 657, 963, 1411, 2068, 3031, 4442, 6510, 9541, 13983, 20493, 30034, 44017, 64510, 945 ...

PUZZLE 97

Having bought a helium balloon for your daughter's birthday, you have to drive home quickly from the shop to reach her party on time. You tie the balloon to a seat and, since it is a cold day outside, you close all the windows.

When you drive around a tight sweeping curve in the road, which way does the balloon swing, towards the inside of the road curve, or away from it. ?

PUZZLE 98

Can you find the odd-one-out between these four trees ?

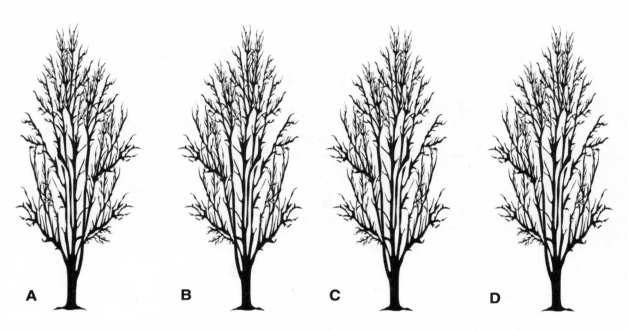

A   B   C   D

PUZZLE 99

This one is not as easy as it looks. Can you see how many triangles are here ?

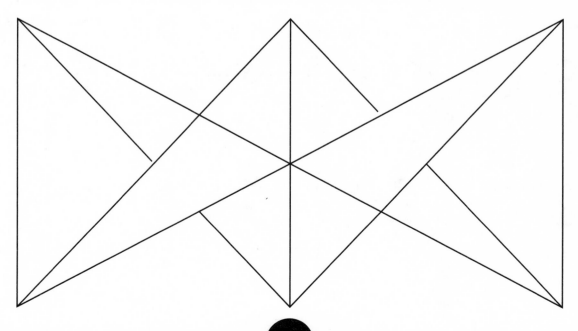

PUZZLE 100

Can you work out the value of the symbols, and hence the missing value ?

     23

     10

     18

PUZZLE 101

Can you work out the minimum whole number value missing from the last set of scales?

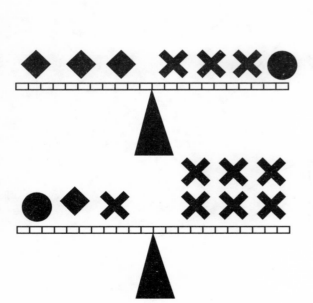

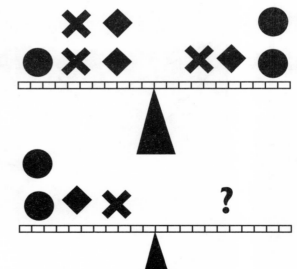

PUZZLE 102

Good at anagrams ? 1 across is an anagram. Solve it to provide you with the first letter of each vertical column. Although the rows have been shuffled, apart from row 1, the letters in the rows have not been shuffled, so if you solve 1 across and any of the downward clues, you will easily solve the whole puzzle.

Across

1. Could mean a ball, or something false.

Down

1: There is no action without this.
2. Help to resolve something.
3. Goes both up and down.

4. Perhaps an expression of doubt.
5. No-one asked for this.
6. A vision of beauty could do this to you.
7. The purpose of caricature.
8. Citizen of the star.
9. The easiest way to go.
10. Non-conventional adventure.

	1	2	3	4	5	6	7	8	9	10
1	A	E	U	A	E	M	Q	R	S	D
	E	S	W	I	D	N	U	C	I	A
	V	A	A	E	B	T	D	E	W	C
	T	S	Y	N	N	E	E	N	L	E
	M	Y	R	T	D	A	C	I	H	P
	E	L	I	S	I	R	I	R	N	A
	N	I	A	O	E	C	L	A	L	D
	O	N	T	U	N	N	I	M	O	S

	1	2	3	4	5	6	7	8	9	10
1										

PUZZLE 103

Can you figure out the missing number in wheel C ?

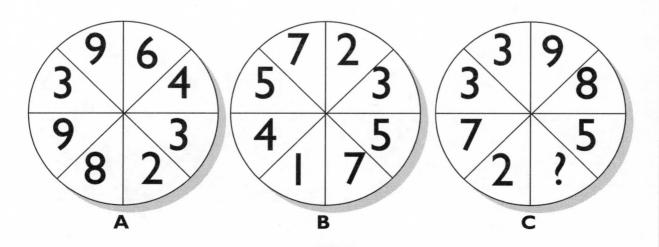

A   B   C

PUZZLE 104

Can you assemble the following components to make a rectangle ?

PUZZLE 105

In each row of the grid below, the nickname of an American State is concealed. The real names of the states are alongside the codekey. Use the key to decode the nicknames. There is an added complication in that the letter A , B, C & D can be represented respectively by either 1, 2, 3, 4 or 3, 4, 5, 6 but the same letter is not represented by a different number on the same line. Each dash stands for a missing letter

A	2	2	5	6	1	1	2	6	6	3	2	2	3	5	6	1

B	4	3	1	2	5	1	3	6	4	5	2	5	3	6	1	2

C	2	2	3	2	1	5	1	1	2	3	2	5	4	5	5	1

D	1	1	5	5	1	6	3	2	1	1	2	1	2	5	1	1

E	2	1	5	5	5	1	5	1	2	1	2	5	5	5	1	3

F	4	1	3	1	3	4	2	5	6	1	2	3	2	5	1	4

– – – – – – – **Alaska**
– – – – – – – **California**
– – – – – – – **Connecticut**
– – – – – – **Hawaii**
– – – – – – **Iowa**
– – – – – – – **Minnesota**

	1	2	3	4	5	6
	a	b	c	d	e	f
	g	h	i	j	k	l
	m	n	o	p	q	r
	s	t	u	v	w	x
	y	z	a	b	c	d

58

PUZZLE 106

One of these split balls does not go with the others. Can you pick it out ?

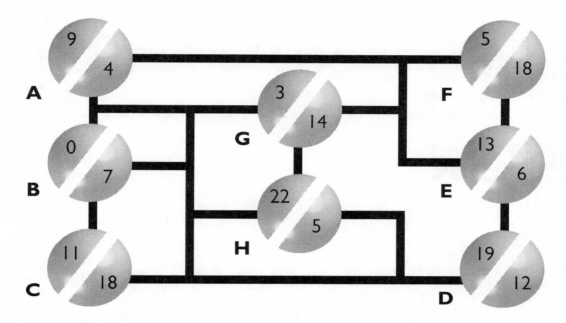

PUZZLE 107

A single black dot is missing from this diagram. Can you mark it in ?

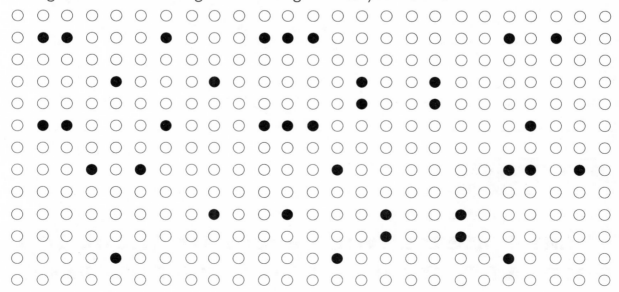

PUZZLE 108

Can you solve the following anagrammatic sentence to find a famous saying by James Russell Lowell ? In most, but not all cases, the anagram words are whole anagrams.

HTE MOISTENS FUR THREADS TO BARE RAE ETHOS TTAH NERVE MECO

PUZZLE 109

Can you find the number that should go in the middle of figure C ?

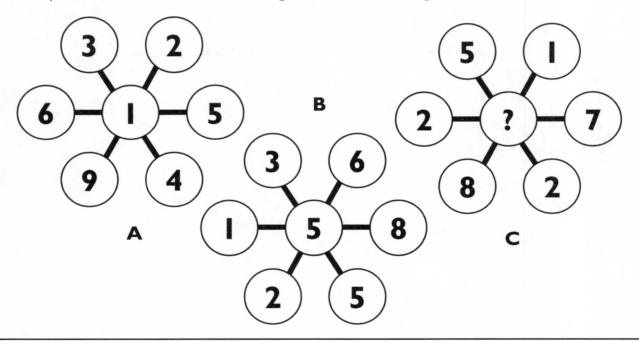

PUZZLE 110

What appears twice every moment and once every minute, but never appears in a thousand years ?

PUZZLE 111

Which is the only cube shown here that can be made from this layout?

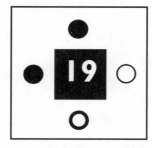 

PUZZLE 112

Can you figure out what should go in the middle of the last square ?

PUZZLE 113

Can you work out the value of the symbols, and hence the missing value ?

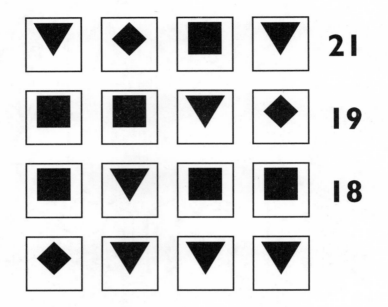

PUZZLE 114

A tragic plane crash happened exactly on the border between USA and Canada. The search teams took ages to reach the plane because the location was remote. Before the flight, everyone had written their last will and testament, declaring preferred place of burial. Fifteen of the those on board were French, but only eight of those wanted to be buried in France, the rest preferring Canada. Twenty-five were Canadian, but sixteen of those wanted to be buried in France, the rest preferring the USA. Forty of the passengers were American, but five of those preferred to be buried in France, and two in Canada.

Where were most of the survivors buried ?

PUZZLE 115

Can you find ten differences in B ?

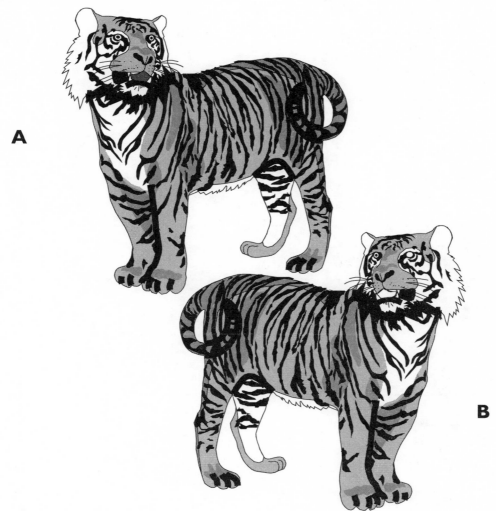

A

B

PUZZLE 116

Can you find the next number in this sequence ?

33, 36, 42, 44, 48, 56, ...

PUZZLE 117

The dial represents an old fashioned telephone dial, with letters and numbers. Beside it is a list of carnivores. Can you find all of them using the dial to decode the list ?

A	4355
B	30251
C	73326
D	55535572
E	4256162
F	259
G	9342117
H	226627
I	1322713
J	6157326

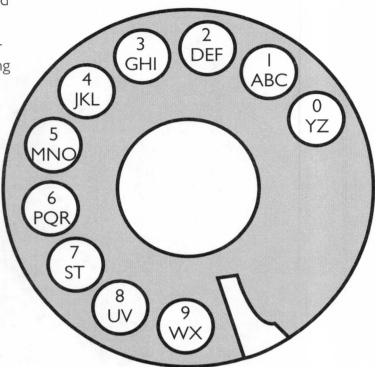

PUZZLE 118

What do you throw out when you want to use it, but take in when you don't want to use it ?

PUZZLE 119

Can you work out which tile set goes into the middle of this panel ?

a	s	d	f	g	h	j	k	l	m	n	o	i	z	x	v	c
x	v	c	a	s	d	f	g	h	j	k	l	m	n	o	i	z
o	i	z	x	v	c	a	s	d	f	g	h	j	k	l	m	n
l	m	n	o	i	z	x	v	c	a	s	d	f	g	h	j	k
h	j	k	l	m	n	o	i	z	x	v	c	a	s	d	f	g
d	f	g	h	j	k	l	m		o	i	z	x	v	c	a	s
c	a	s	d	f	g	h		l	m	n	o	i	z	x	v
z	x	v	c	a	s	d	f		j	k	l	m	n	o	i
n	o	i	z	x	v	c		d	f	g	h	j	k	l	m
k	l	m	n	o	i	z	x		a	s	d	f	g	h	i
g	h	j	k	l	m	n	o		z	x	v	c	a	s	d	f
s	d	f	g	h	j	k	l	m	n	o	i	z	x	v	c	a
v	c	a	s	d	f	g	h	j	k	l	m	n	o	i	z	x
i	z	x	v	c	a	s	d	f	g	h	j	k	l	m	n	o
m	n	o	i	z	x	v	c	a	s	d	f	g	h	j	k	l
j	k	l	m	n	o	i	z	x	v	c	a	s	d	f	g	h
f	g	h	j	k	l	m	n	o	i	z	x	v	c	a	s	d

A

	n	
j	k	
	g	h
a	s	
	v	c
	i	

B

	n	
k	j	
	g	h
a	s	
	i	v
	c	

C

	n	
j	k	
	g	h
a	s	
	c	i
	v	

D

	n	
j	k	
	g	h
i	s	
	v	c
	a	

65

PUZZLE 120

How many circles does it take to balance the three crosses ?

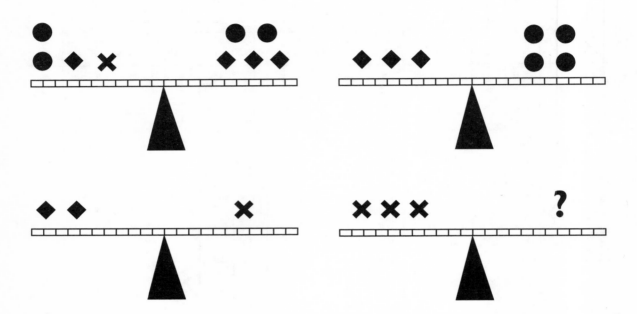

PUZZLE 121

Can you figure out what letter should replace the question mark ?

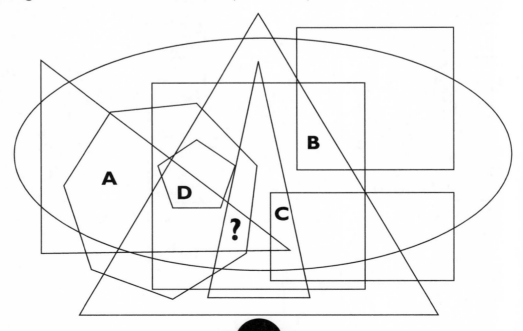

PUZZLE 122

Can you work out the missing number in wheel C ?

A

B

C

PUZZLE 123

How much earth can be excavated from a hole 6 feet wide, 3 feet long, and 2 feet 6 inches deep?

PUZZLE 124

Can you see which set (A & A1, B & B1 or C & C1), are not true mirror-images ?

PUZZLE 125

What is the next number in the sequence?

8, 12, 18, 27, 40.5, ...

PUZZLE 126

Four of these components can be fitted together to make a rectangle, and one of the components is not required. Can you fit the pieces together and say which piece is extra?

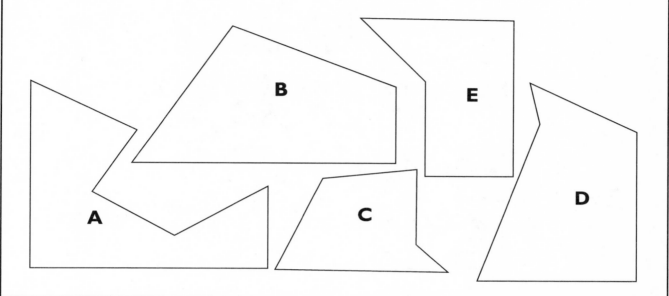

PUZZLE 127

Can you solve the anagrams to find the inventors of the following items: Bifocal Lens, Electric Light, Microphone, Chain Drive, Adding Machine, Revolver, Vulcanized Rubber, Jet Engine. (Where there is dispute about the inventor, the best known has been used, excluding titles such as Sir.... Each name is on a separate line. Some middle names are included.

CAPABLE SAILS
BLANK INNER FIN JAM
MOST ADHESION
LEARNED BALL HEXAGRAM
LAME LOCUST
ADORES HOLY GRACE
THREW FLAT INK
DIVORCED IN A LOAN

PUZZLE 128

Can you work out the value of the symbols, and hence the missing value ?

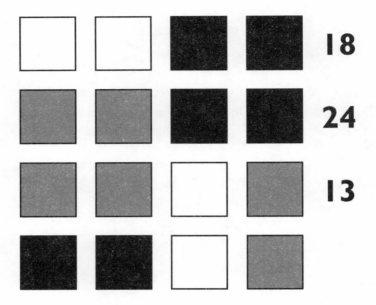

PUZZLE 129

Can you find the odd-one-out between these five cubes ?

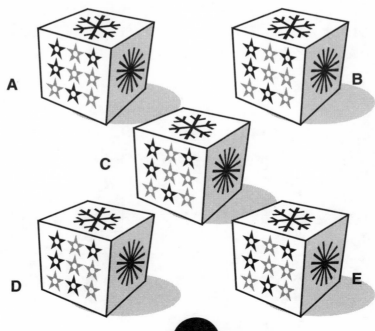

PUZZLE 130

Can you figure out what should go in the middle of box C ?

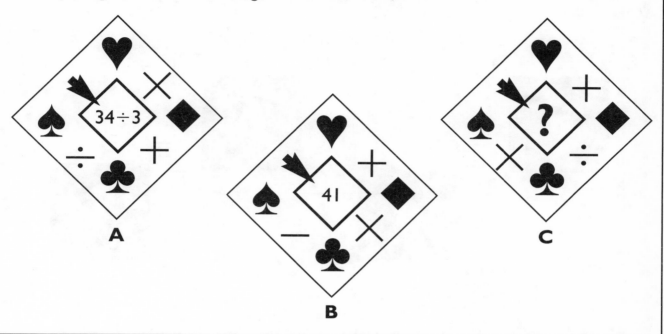

A

B

C

PUZZLE 131

What can go up a chimney down, but never go down a chimney up?

PUZZLE 132

Can you work out what number should go into the last square ?

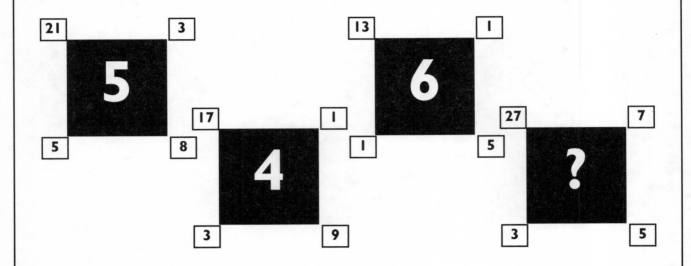

PUZZLE 133

Can you figure out what number should go in place of the question mark? Hint: opposite pairings are related in some way.

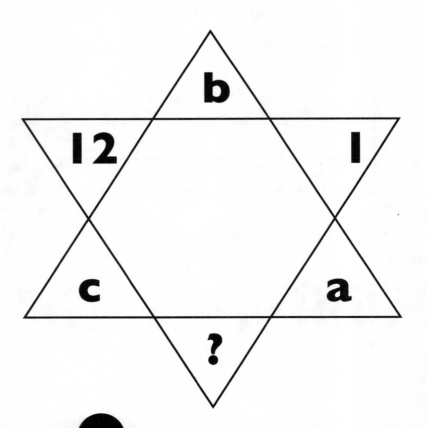

PUZZLE 134

What kind of key do you often find at the beach?

PUZZLE 135

In each row of the grid below, a girl's name is concealed. Use the key provided to decode the names. There is an added complication in that the letter A may be represented by either 1, or 9, or both.

1	2	3	4	5	6	7	8	9
a	b	c	d	e	f	g	h	i
j	k	l	m	n	o	p	q	r
s	t	u	v	w	x	y	z	a

A | 8 | 2 | 2 | 3 | 8 | 4 | 1 | 5 | 4 | 7 | 4 | 3 | 8 | 1 | 9 | 8

B | 7 | 4 | 1 | 5 | 9 | 5 | 3 | 3 | 5 | 4 | 5 | 3 | 5 | 4 | 6 | 3

C | 2 | 4 | 9 | 4 | 1 | 3 | 1 | 1 | 5 | 4 | 3 | 8 | 5 | 3 | 8 | 2

D | 3 | 9 | 7 | 4 | 8 | 5 | 1 | 2 | 8 | 5 | 9 | 4 | 5 | 4 | 1 | 3

E | 4 | 3 | 4 | 5 | 9 | 3 | 6 | 3 | 1 | 1 | 2 | 6 | 9 | 1 | 5 | 5

F | 4 | 3 | 6 | 4 | 6 | 9 | 1 | 6 | 6 | 3 | 3 | 6 | 9 | 5 | 1 | 1

PUZZLE 136

All of the words in this grid are connected to police activity surrounding a crime. Can you find them ? Words may be written in a straight line in any direction, backwards, forwards, diagonally, up or down.

FORENSIC SCIENCE, CRIME SCENE, ARREST,
EVIDENCE, MAGNIFYING GLASS, FOOTPRINTS,
CLUES, DNA TESTING, WEAPON,
CULPABILITY, INVESTIGATION, SUSPECT.
POLICE, COURT,

S	S	A	L	G	G	N	I	Y	F	I	N	G	A	M	L	A
T	A	P	P	O	R	S	L	U	N	K	M	U	R	F	R	Y
N	F	O	O	T	P	R	I	N	T	S	C	A	N	R	T	I
I	F	A	N	I	W	U	N	O	R	E	B	L	E	O	N	P
R	U	O	N	F	R	A	S	C	A	U	L	S	C	R	I	O
P	M	I	R	N	A	L	P	E	R	L	T	P	I	T	R	L
R	A	T	O	E	V	I	D	E	N	C	E	R	D	E	T	I
E	E	C	T	I	N	V	E	N	E	C	S	E	M	I	R	C
G	S	W	T	A	T	S	E	A	K	P	I	O	C	L	E	E
N	I	N	V	E	S	T	I	G	A	T	I	O	N	T	E	A
I	M	H	W	A	S	E	O	C	Y	H	C	S	T	E	E	T
F	I	G	A	E	R	S	N	H	S	O	T	E	O	O	M	D
Y	T	I	L	I	B	A	P	L	U	C	F	O	P	Y	E	N
R	O	L	D	T	Y	A	E	R	H	T	I	E	P	S	O	R
E	I	V	R	I	N	B	G	Y	I	T	A	E	W	A	U	G
Y	T	U	E	H	G	N	I	T	S	E	T	A	N	D	B	S
T	O	T	N	I	O	A	D	A	L	W	T	E	K	C	C	U
C	L	I	E	H	N	O	P	A	E	W	T	T	N	I	E	W

PUZZLE 137

Can you work out which tile set goes into the middle of this panel ?

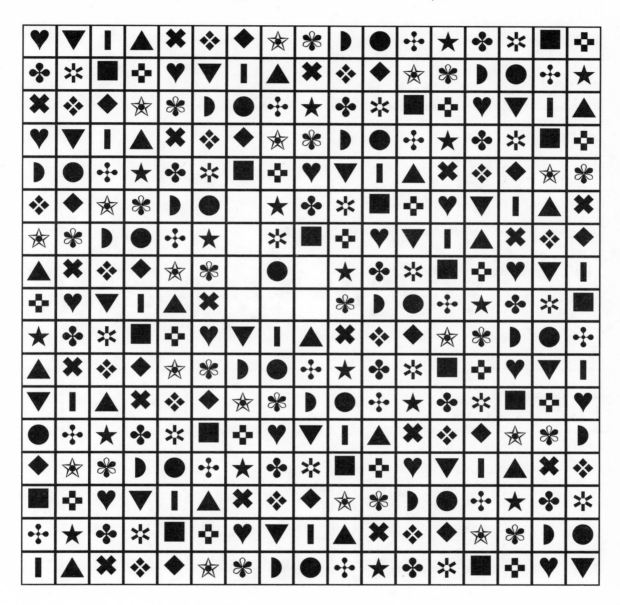

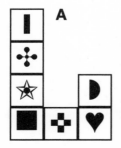
A

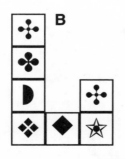
B

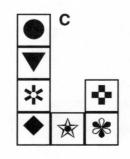
C

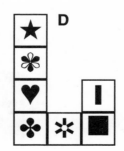
D

PUZZLE 138

What value should replace the question mark?

PUZZLE 139

Can you find the missing number in this sequence ?

..., 81, 54, 36, 24, 16

PUZZLE 140

Can you work out the value of the bottom line ?

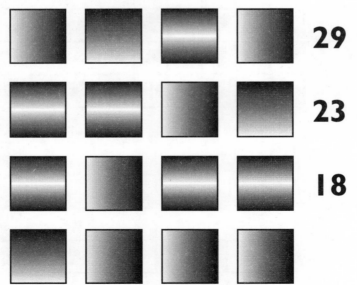

29

23

18

PUZZLE 141

Can you find the anagrams of the official names for phobias of the following :
Each is one word, ending in '...phobia', and starts with the letter in square brackets after the clue.
Each is on a separate line.

YOUNG GIRLS [P], WORDS [L], TEETH [D], GOING TO BED [C],
STRING [L], MONSTERS [T], SKIN [D], CLOUDS [N]

HIPPO HEBONA	**BEAT AIR PHOTO**
OH NO I BATH PAPER	**A NOON HIP BOIL**
PONCHO ALIBI	**A BIOMORPH DATE**
A BIG LOO HOP	**BOP IT ON A HOOD**

PUZZLE 142

Can you find ten differences between Fred and his twin brother Joe ?

Fred   **Joe**

PUZZLE 143

This problem has two parts.

a. Solve this anagram to find a rather strange four word theological question.
b. Apart from the obvious, what do you find unusual about this question ?

EGO SEEDED EGOS ?

PUZZLE 144

Can you decipher the following strange code to find a famous quote by Thomas Edison ? Words are separated by spaces. (Eg: There are three words in the 1st line.) Each symbol always stands for the same letter. The end of each line is the end of a word, and the following words are part of the sentence, but in a mixed up order.

by inventions anything never doing accident my worth

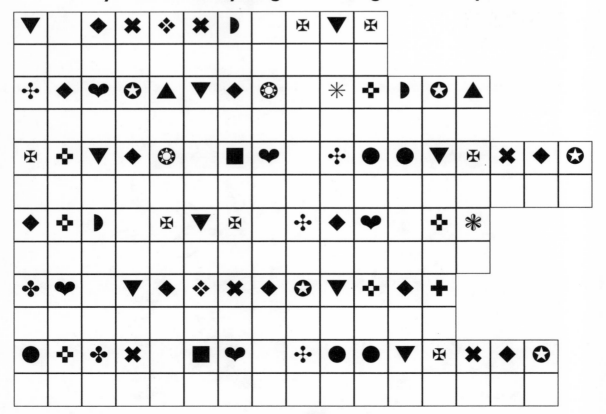

PUZZLE 145

Can you figure out what value balances these symbols ?

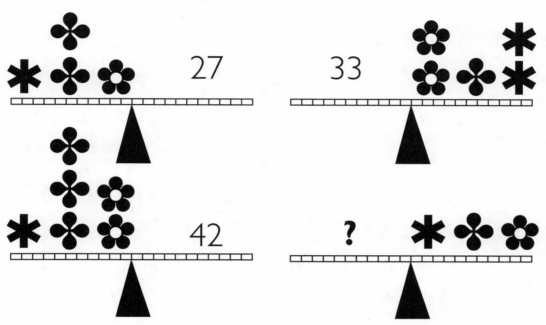

27

33

42

?

PUZZLE 146

Can you find the missing number ?

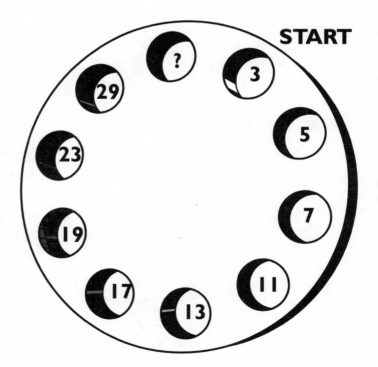

START

PUZZLE 147

Somewhere within this grid is a 4 x 4 block in which every row, column, and long diagonal adds to 38. Can you find it ?

2	5	10	14	2	5	10	14	2	5	10	14	2
6	17	13	9	6	17	13	9	6	17	11	9	6
14	2	13	9	14	2	13	9	14	2	13	9	14
10	16	7	4	11	16	7	4	11	16	7	4	10
15	3	8	12	15	3	8	12	15	3	8	12	15
17	5	10	6	17	5	10	6	17	5	11	6	17
3	15	8	12	3	15	8	12	3	15	8	12	3
14	2	7	9	14	2	13	9	14	2	13	9	14
4	16	13	11	4	16	7	11	4	16	7	13	4
3	15	8	12	3	15	8	12	3	15	8	12	3
10	5	10	6	17	5	10	6	17	5	17	6	10

PUZZLE 148

Can you work out the central value to replace the question mark ?

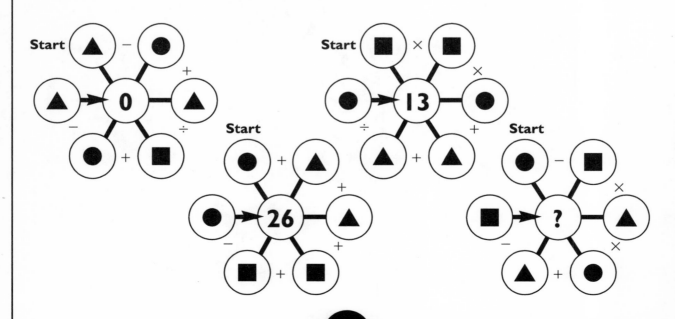

PUZZLE 149

In the far reaches of space there is an infinite hotel that has an infinite number of rooms, all containing long term guests who intend to stay forever. One day the manager gets a phone call booking in an infinite number of new guests, each of whom will require a single room.

Can the manager take the booking, and if so, which room numbers will he assign to his new guests ?

PUZZLE 150

How many ellipses enclose the black dot?

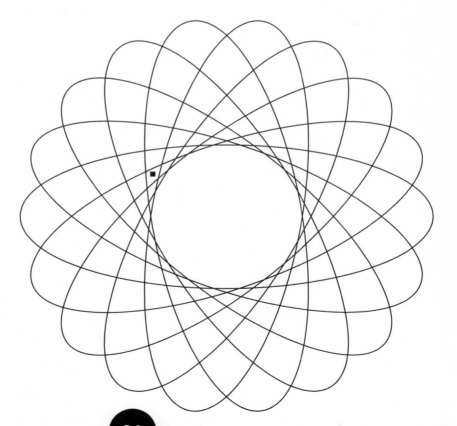

PUZZLE 151

Can you find the next number in this sequence ?

1, 1, 2, 4, 7, 13, 24, ...

PUZZLE 152

Can you figure out what number should go in the middle of the bottom star ?

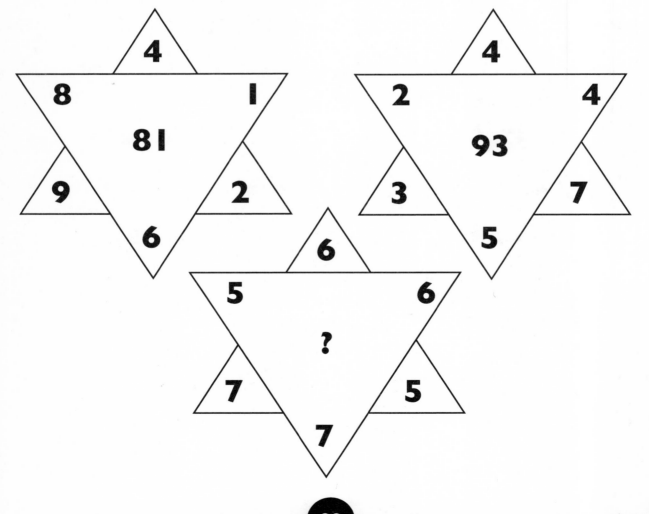

PUZZLE 153

This is one anagram containing eight words related to self-esteem and personal value. The words have been run together, so the end of a line here may not be the end of a word. Can you find the words ? Clue : Each of the words has a similar meaning to one of the following words, (but they are not in this order):

joy; prosperity; fitness; strength; ingenuity; certainty; liberty; peace.

**ESCUSSCOMDEREFWOPREN
HYMOARLHTAHEHSPAPSINE
TRAVYEICITNODIEENFCC**

PUZZLE 154

can you work out the missing value ?

 14

 10

 6

PUZZLE 155

Can you figure out how to fit these shapes together to make a rectangle ?

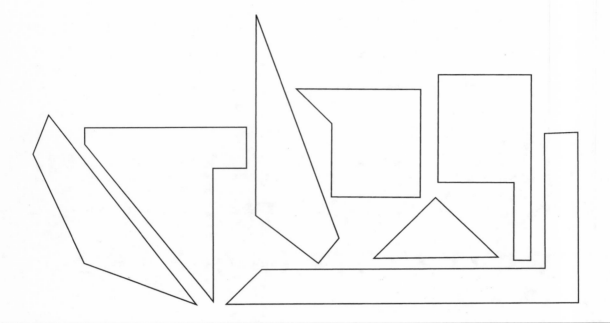

PUZZLE 156

When Maggie arrives at work alone, she must walk up the stairs, but when she arrives with a friend she can use the elevator.
Why ?

Hint: It's not because of any rule or regulation.

PUZZLE 157

Can you work out which tile set goes into the middle of this panel ?

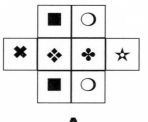

A

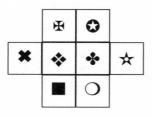

B

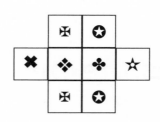

C

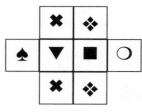

D

PUZZLE 158

Can you find the solution to this analogy ?

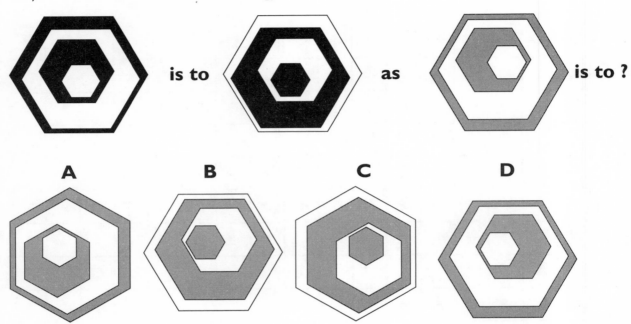

PUZZLE 159

I'm thinking of a number that, when I multiply it by two and divide the result by four, then multiply the result of that by itself, gives me a number that, when I subtract four and divide the result by ten, gives me six.

What was the number I originally thought of ?

PUZZLE 160

Can you solve this anagram to find a single word that means the same as unbiased ?

TINY RAID ON MICRONS

PUZZLE 161

Which linked pair of balls does not go with the other two pairs.

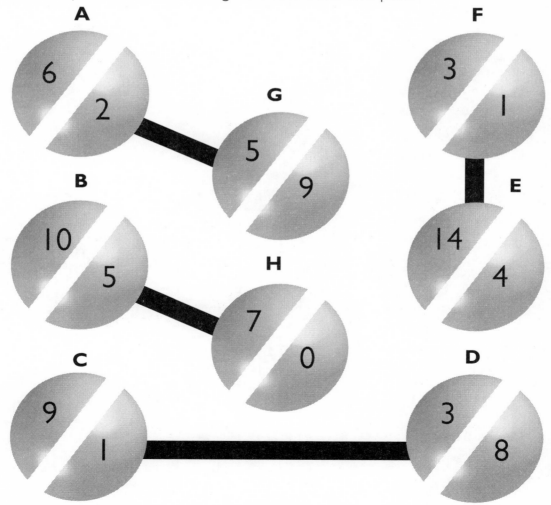

PUZZLE 162

Can you spot 10 differences in B ?

A

B

PUZZLE 163

In each row of the grid below, is a word which solves the following anagrams, which are all connected with personal qualities :
A. OGREUCA; B. AHIRYCT; C. OEHP; D. RCGEA; E. TAPIEENC; F. RPNIHSEIFD.

Can you use the key to find the words ? There is an added complication in that the letters A , & B, can be represented respectively by either 1, & 2, or 6 & 7, but the same letter is not represented by a different number on the same line.

1	2	3	4	5	6	7
a	b	c	d	e	f	g
h	i	j	k	l	m	n
o	p	q	r	s	t	u
v	w	x	y	z	a	b

A

5	2	3	1	7	4	6	7	5	1	4	5	5	1	2	3

B

7	5	6	4	6	3	1	6	4	2	6	4	5	6	4	1

C

3	1	1	8	9	5	4	1	1	2	5	7	3	3	4	6

D

1	2	8	3	9	7	4	6	3	5	2	4	2	4	1	1

E

2	1	6	2	5	7	3	5	5	6	2	4	1	3	4	5

F

1	3	2	6	4	2	5	7	4	5	1	2	2	7	1	7

PUZZLE 164

Can you work out the missing number in wheel C ?

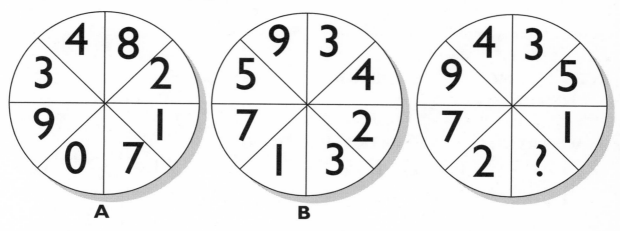

A   B

PUZZLE 165

Can you reassemble these block pairs into the correct place in this square to make each row, column, and long diagonal add to 40 ?

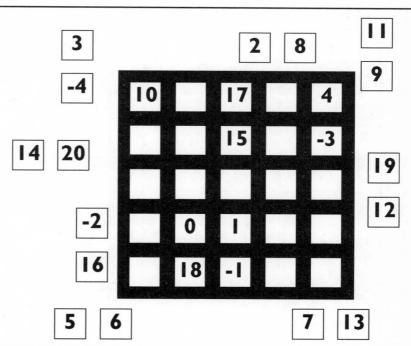

PUZZLE 166

At crossroads on a journey, is it better to ask a compulsive liar the way to go, or to ask somebody who lies only occasionally ?

PUZZLE 167

In this grid, the ten words related to things that are useful to have for puzzle solving may go up, down, along, backwards or forwards, or diagonally, but they all have at least one bend somewhere.

Can you find the following ten words in the grid ?

INTELLIGENCE, THINKING, HEAD, IMAGINATION, MEMORY, CLARITY, PLANNING, INTROSPECTION, CREATIVITY, FORESIGHT.

A	E	S	B	M	K	L	P	O	I	C	U	T	Y	R	E	W
S	E	F	R	F	G	T	H	L	R	K	J	H	G	F	D	A
U	H	I	B	N	M	O	P	E	I	B	G	Y	D	L	K	G
Y	J	H	N	G	T	T	A	F	X	Z	W	E	E	R	T	R
P	O	I	U	T	G	I	U	I	J	Y	N	C	O	O	J	J
J	H	Y	U	H	E	Y	V	K	T	K	N	L	T	U	I	U
F	K	O	H	I	B	L	E	I	S	E	O	A	G	F	H	O
O	I	S	E	N	S	K	L	S	G	K	Q	R	I	T	Y	K
R	G	N	I	K	U	I	E	I	S	O	C	K	S	Q	E	L
E	O	I	U	C	L	Q	M	S	Y	V	W	G	U	C	I	U
S	I	G	H	T	W	A	L	K	E	R	F	N	E	K	Q	K
C	U	E	L	Q	G	F	U	Y	H	G	O	V	M	P	L	F
W	I	O	K	I	V	I	H	S	W	I	U	M	E	I	S	C
K	S	L	V	N	O	K	N	F	T	V	M	C	O	K	Q	O
O	U	E	N	U	I	W	O	A	S	E	T	S	U	C	R	E
C	W	A	O	E	Q	N	E	L	M	I	O	Q	V	T	W	U
Q	L	O	C	I	G	H	F	A	O	L	C	K	N	L	E	Q
P	U	S	K	U	E	I	S	K	D	N	E	I	O	I	S	K

PUZZLE 168

Can you figure out what number should go in the last square ?

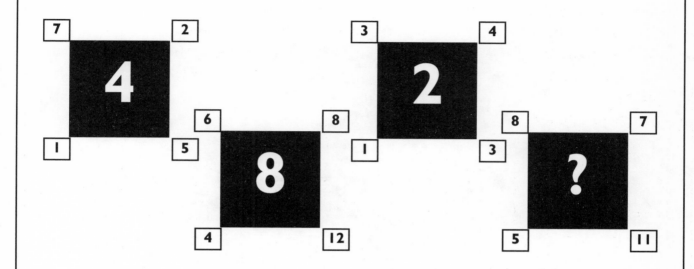

PUZZLE 169

Can you find the missing number ?

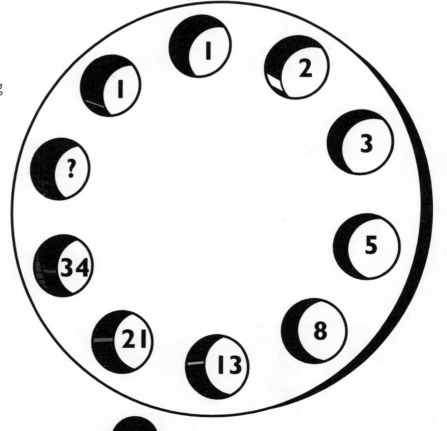

PUZZLE 170

Can you solve these anagrams to find a famous 13 word motivational statement about success by Scott Flansburg ? Every two words (except the last) of the quotation have been combined in anagram, and given a separate line.

**WHERE YOUTH
INK YOUTH
ACORN
ON BET CAN
FUSSY LOCUS CUE
ILL WEB
GIRTH**

PUZZLE 171

Can you figure out the missing value ?

12

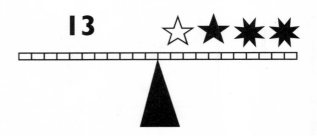
13

13

?

PUZZLE 172

I'm thinking of a number that, when I multiply it by two and subtract eight from the result, then divide the result of that by five, gives me a number that, when I multiply it by itself and subtract the result of that from one hundred, gives me a solution that, when divided by eight, gives eight.

What was the number I originally thought of ?

PUZZLE 173

Can you solve this anagram to find a word that means the same as accompaniment ?

TO CONMAN TIC

PUZZLE 174

Can you work out the missing value ?

    25

    28

    14

PUZZLE 175

Can you decipher the following cryptic code to find a famous saying by Emile Coué ? Words are separated by spaces. (Eg: There are four words in the 1st line.) Each symbol always stands for the same letter. The end of each line is the end of a word, and some, but not all of the following words are part of the sentence, in a mixed up order.

better, being, by, quick, every, living, getting, love, I'm, day, and.

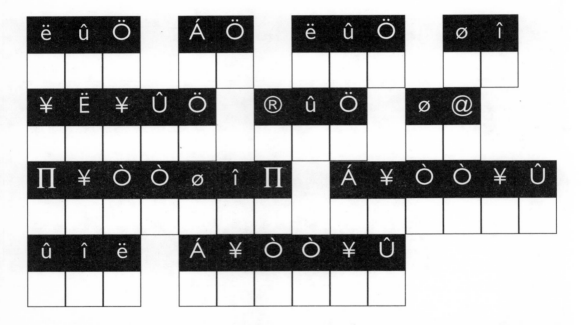

PUZZLE 176

Can you work out what comes next in this sequence ?

A, S, O, N, D, J, F, ...

PUZZLE 177

Can you find, hidden within this grid, a 5 x 5 square in which the totals in all horizontal, vertical, and long diagonals add to 20 ?

3	2	9	3	1	9	5	2	5	2	1	9	3	5	1	3	2	9
9	5	2	2	9	5	3	1	1	5	3	2	9	1	3	9	5	2
5	3	1	3	1	9	5	2	2	9	5	3	1	2	9	5	3	1
9	5	2	5	2	1	9	3	3	1	9	5	2	3	1	3	9	2
2	1	5	3	9	2	1	5	1	3	9	5	2	3	9	2	1	5
3	2	9	5	1	3	2	9	3	9	2	5	1	5	1	3	2	9
5	3	1	9	2	5	3	1	5	1	3	9	2	9	2	5	3	1
9	5	2	1	3	9	5	2	9	2	5	1	3	1	3	9	5	2
1	9	3	2	5	1	9	3	1	3	9	2	5	2	5	1	9	3
2	1	5	2	9	5	3	1	2	5	1	3	9	3	9	2	1	5
3	2	9	3	1	9	5	2	5	2	1	9	3	5	1	3	2	9
5	3	1	5	2	1	9	3	9	3	2	1	5	9	2	5	3	1
9	5	2	2	9	5	3	1	1	5	3	2	9	1	3	9	5	2
5	3	1	3	1	9	5	2	2	9	5	3	1	2	9	5	3	1
9	5	2	5	2	1	9	3	3	1	9	5	2	3	1	3	9	2
1	9	3	1	3	9	5	2	5	2	5	2	1	9	3	1	9	3

PUZZLE 178

What bears white fruit, has deep, deep roots, but watered, never grows new shoots ?

PUZZLE 179

Can you work out what comes next in this sequence ?

ST, ET, NT, TW, TO, TT, ...

PUZZLE 180

Can you work out which tile set goes into the middle of this panel ?

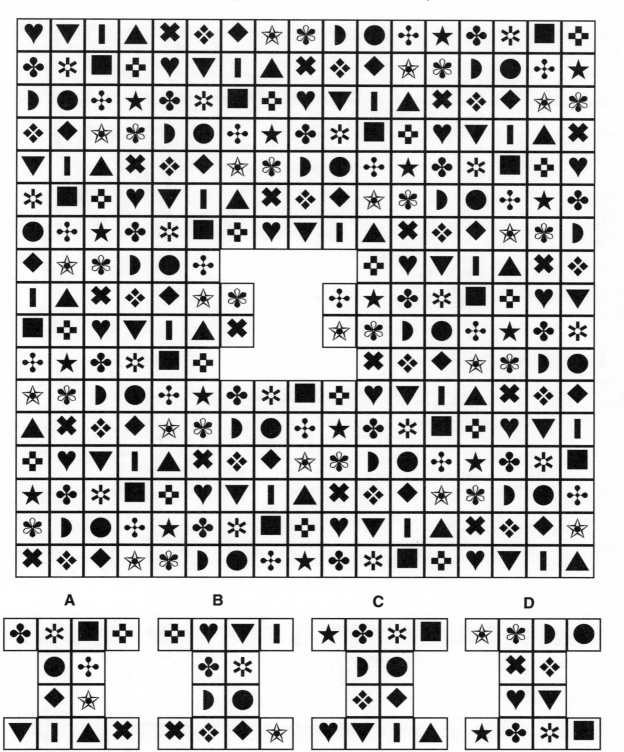

A   B   C   D

1. D

2. 13. The bottom right numbers in each circle are the sum of the other three numbers.

3. A. The middle symbol is always the same shape as the most common outer symbol.

4. A watch with a second hand.

5. s. The letters stand for days of the week, starting with Tuesday, and ending with s for Sunday.

6. B

7. There are seven: Mon..days, Tues..days... Wednes..days....

8. 15. The numbers are all odd, and rise in two sets, 1, 3, 5, 7 & 9, 11, 13 & [15].

9.

30	39	48	1	10	19	28
38	47	7	9	18	27	29
46	6	8	17	26	35	37
5	14	16	25	34	36	45
13	15	24	33	42	44	4
21	23	32	41	43	3	12
22	31	40	49	2	11	20

10. Yugoslavia, Australia, Scotland, Russia, Honduras, South Africa, Germany, Barbados.

11. 4. There are 4 overlapping shapes at this point.

12. 52. 9 × 3 × 2 (- 2) = 52

13. It contains every letter of the alphabet.

14. First cut the lines down the middle. Then slide one half down until the position of the first line in one half meets with the second line in the other half. Thus 10 lines become 9 slightly longer lines.

15. 5:45. Each clock progressively adds 35 minutes.

16. E is the next logical step.

17. Because seven ate nine!

18. B. Minimum whole number values are:

● 3 ◆ 4 ✖ 2

19. 119. All others have a first single digit and then a double digit that together add to 16.

20.

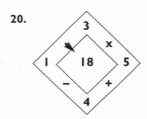

21. The Beatles, The Rolling Stones, Mike and the Mechanics, Fleetwood Mac, Pink Floyd, Dire Straits.

22. A. Paris, B. Lisbon, C. London, D. New York, E. Sidney, F. Rome, G. Marseilles, H. Milan, I. Tokyo, J. Athens.

23. E. There is one less bit on this clown's tie.

24. A

25. H.

26. policy cash log is an anagram of psychological which has the same meaning.

27. The cities are shown in the grid below.

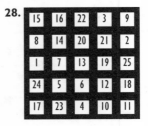

28.

15	16	22	3	9
8	14	20	21	2
1	7	13	19	25
24	5	6	12	18
17	23	4	10	11

29. The solutions are given here in the same position as in the question.

hydrogen   nitrogen
phosphorus   chlorine
titanium   arsenic
manganese   magnesium

30. The black spot should be placed in the bottom row fifth from the right. In each row, the position of the first two black spots, counting from the left, added together, equals the position of the right-hand spot on that line. Thus, 5 + 8 = 13.

31. They had failed to put a ladder down the side of the yacht and were unable to climb back in. They were not strong enough to swim two hundred miles back to shore, so they drowned.

32. a.

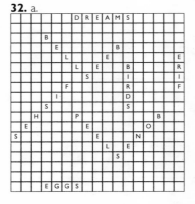

b.
BELLS	CAMPANOLOGY
FISHES	ICHTHYOLOGY
BEES	APIOLOGY
SLEEP	HYPNOLOGY
BIRDS	ORNITHOLOGY
BONES	OSTEOLOGY
DREAMS	ONEIRILOGY
EGGS	OOLOGY
FIRE	PYROLOGY

33. 3. Starting from the top, 7+2=9; then take the left and right numbers, combine them, and divide by that 9, thus 2&7=27; 27/9=3.

34. Z. Map the numbers from 3 to 13 against the diametrically opposite letters from p to z.

35. At the most, if it were a square forest and the dog stuck to the diagonal, he could run just over 35.35 miles into the forest, and he would do that on the first day. After that, he would start running out of the forest, since a 2500 square mile, square forest, is 50 × 50 miles.

36. D. Each cube has below it the answer to the question, 'Is this a perfect square ?'
Since D says 'No' and yet it is a perfect square (7 × 7), it is the only cube wrongly labelled.

37. q. Start with c in the top left of A and fill in the segments by reading down diagonals, as in the table below. In B we would finish with n, r, m, and move to the next circle with q, u, p...etc.

38. D.
There is an extra one of these: ✥

39. C. There is no area in this set enclosed by all three components, unlike in the others.

40. Immediately eat the first paper you pick out of the box. That way, the Board will be forced to examine the remaining paper. They will decide that you must have eaten the paper with "yes" on it, and you will be accepted onto the Board.

41. A. Bach; B. Haydn; C. Mozart; D. Wagner; E. Mahler; F. Schubert; G. Stravinski; H. Toscanini; I. Bruckner; J. Tchaikovski.

42. 7. Multiply the two bottom numbers together and add, in an anti-clockwise direction, the next three numbers to the total.

43. The remains of a melted snowman.

44. The hands of the clocks are pointing to numbers for simple addition. In the top row, 9+12=17; 7+1=10. In the bottom row, 4+12=16; 11+5=16.

45. George Washington, Richard Milhouse Nixon, William McKinley, Theodore Roosevelt, Calvin Coolidge, Chester Alan Arthur, Lyndon Baines Johnson.

46.
3	5	6	1	9
6	1	9	3	5
9	3	5	6	1
5	6	1	9	3
1	9	3	5	6

47.
T	H	E		S	U	B	L	I	M	E		A	N	D		T
H	E		R	I	D	I	C	U	L	O	U	S		A	R	E
O	F	T	E	N		S	O		N	E	A	R	L	Y		R
E	L	A	T	E	D		T	H	A	T		I	T		I	S
D	I	F	F	I	C	U	L	T		T	O		C	L	A	S
S		T	H	E	M		S	E	P	A	R	A	T	E	L	Y
O	N	E		S	T	E	P		A	B	O	V	E		T	H
E		S	U	B	L	I	M	E		M	A	K	E	S		T
H	E		R	I	D	I	C	U	L	O	U	S		A	N	D
O	N	E		S	T	E	P		A	B	O	V	E		T	H
E		R	I	D	I	C	U	L	O	U	S		M	A	K	E
S		T	H	E		S	U	B	L	I	M	E		A	G	A
I	N	-	T	H	O	M	A	S		P	A	I	N	E		

48. C.

49. Push the cork into the bottle and shake the coin out.

50. 7. In each wheel, the total of the top half equals the total of the bottom half.

51. B.

52. The letter 'e'.

53.

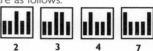

Thus, 14 + 17 = 31.

54. 17. The values of each barcode are as follows.

2	3	4	7

55. 17.

56. 4. The values are shown below.
♥ 2 ◆ 3 ♣ 4 ♠ 5

57. Here is the sentence with the correct spacing:
A hdlic acn sak a dtushaon snueosqit ttah teh tswies nma toncna sarewn.
And here is the solution:
A child can ask a thousand questions that the wisest man cannot answer.

58. 35. From the left, the numbers are 12 × 12 (-1), 11 × 11 (-1), 10 × 10 (-1), 9 × 9 (-1), 8 × 8 (-1), 7 × 7 (-1), and 6 × 6 (-1) = 35.

59. Lines are through those words that run together, for clarity.

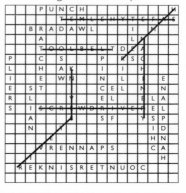

60. D. It is a reflection, not a rotation.

61. 2. Add the top two numbers and subtract the bottom two numbers.

62. 3 crosses.

63. They drowned when their ship crashed into the rocks. Marie-Anne was a lighthouse keeper!

64.

25	24	16	8	49	41	33
34	26	18	17	9	50	42
43	35	27	19	11	10	51
52	44	36	28	20	12	4
5	46	45	37	29	21	13
14	6	47	39	38	30	22
23	15	7	48	40	32	31

65. WILLIAM SHAKESPEARE; THOMAS CARLYLE; SAMUEL JOHNSON; GEOFFREY CHAUCER; JOSEPH CONRAD; CHARLES DICKENS; WILLIAM MAKEPEACE THACKERAY.

66. C. Both the collection of arrows and the triangle rotate 90 degrees counter-clockwise.

67. 1, 5. Starting from the top left, add consecutive numbers and drop any 10's to get the next number. Thus, 8+5 = 13, drop the first 1 to get 3, then add the previous number to the 3. Hence, 3 + 5 = 8; 8 + 3 = 11; 1 + 8 = 9; 9 + 1 = 10; drop the 1 and keep the 0; thus 0 + 9 =9, then 9 + 0 = 9, 9 + 9 = 18; drop the 1, 8 + 9 = 17; drop the 1; 7 + 8 ......etc. up to 7 + 7=14; drop the 1; 7 + 4 = 1[1]; drop the first 1; 1 + 4 = [5].

68. No man has two heads. A man has one head more than no man. Therefore a man has three heads.

69. A. The circled element has been reversed mirror-image fashion.

70. 11. The values are shown below.

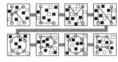

71.

72.

16	3	2	13	15	10	3	6	41	15	14	4	12	8	7	1	12
5	10	11	8	4	5	16	9	9	7	6	12	5	11	10	8	5
9	6	7	12	14	11	2	13	16	3	2	13	15	10	3	6	5
41	15	14	4	12	8	7	1	5	10	11	8	4	5	16	9	15
16	3	2	13	15	10	3	6	15	10	16	2	3	13	16	2	3
5	10	11	8	4	5	16	9	4	5	5	11	10	8	5	11	10
9	6	7	12	14	11	2	13	14	11	9	7	6	12	9	7	6
41	15	14	4	12	8	7	1	12	8	4	14	15	1	14	15	1
9	7	6	12	5	11	10	8	5	11	10	3	6	41	15	14	4
4	14	15	1	9	7	6	12	9	7	5	16	9	9	7	6	12
12	8	13	16	3	4	14	15	1	4	14	11	2	13	16	3	2	13

73. C. There are 4 shapes overlapping at this point, like the other areas marked with C.

74.

	▼	●		●	)	✱	■	◆		◆	■	◆	◆	
	I	T		T	A	K	E	S		L	E	S	S	
●	▼	✚	■		●	▲		◆	▲		◆	✱		
T	I	M	E		T	O		D	O		A			
●	✿	▼	✱	☆		✱	▼	✿	●	●		●	)	✱
T	H	I	N	G		R	I	G	H	T		T	H	A	N
●	▲		■	○	◆	▼	✱					+	○	◆
T	O		E	X	P	L	A	I	N		W	H	Y	
★	▲	▲		◆	▼	◆		▼	●		✚	◆	▲	✱	☆
Y	O	U		D	I	D		I	T		W	R	O	N	G

75. The odd-one-out is E. All others add to 27.

76. Split the balls into 2 sets of 6, and place one set on either side of the scales, to see which side is heavier. Take note of which side. Then, split the heavier set of 6 into 2 and again weigh them. Then, take the heavier set of 3 and weigh two of the balls. If the scales are balanced you know that the remaining ball is the heavier. If they tip, you also know which is heavier.

77.

T				K	D	N	A	H		T	H	G	I	T
R		T	R		E				S				D	
O			I	R				S					R	
U		K		C		S	E	O	H		L	O	V	E	R
S	E	R	S		H			E	L			S	S	
				I	S			I		U	R			
C	O	T	S		E	H			T		P	A		
K				F	I	R	T					E		
I		W	A	I				H				W		
N		S				E	A	T			R			
G			T			S			E		E	D	N	U
S			C		K	U			R					
			O	N		O	L	B	E					
			A		I				I					
			T		C		B	R	A	S	S			
S				K							G	K	S	
R		S	R	E							O			
E	D	N	E	P	S	U	S							

78. Are you dead ?

79. 4. Each number has digits that add to 13.

80. A. Chin dimples are not mirrors of each other.

81. Fascinating; outrageous, alluring, crazy, appealing, trustworthy, seductive, vibrant, delicious, enchanting.

82. C & D. The round spots can be joined to form letters. C & D are out of alphabetical sequence.

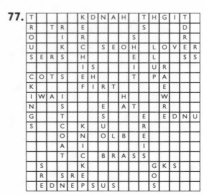

83. 2. This is the only even prime number. Thus, because it is even, it is odd.

84. 14. The values are as below.

◎	3	✳	2	✚	5

85. B. The analogy is for a left-right mirror-image.

86. They fit as below.

87. Two options are possible.

17	9	1	42	34	26	25
8	0	4	13	33	22	24
-1	40	39	31	23	15	7
46	38	30	22	14	6	-2
37	29	21	13	5	4	45
28	20	12	11	3	44	36
19	18	10	2	43	35	27

25	26	34	42	1	9	17
16	24	32	33	41	0	8
7	15	23	31	39	40	-1
-2	6	14	22	30	38	46
45	4	5	13	21	29	37
36	44	3	11	12	20	28
27	35	43	2	10	18	19

88. BROCCOLI, CAULIFLOWER, LETTUCE, ENDIVE, POTATOES, CARROTS, SPINACH, CELERY, SPRING ONIONS, ARTICHOKE, ASPARAGUS, BRUSSELS SPROUTS.

89. Delete the first number to get 19 + 26 = 45.

XIX + XXVI = XLV

90. 7. 4 + 7 = 11; concatenate the 11 to get 2;
2 + 7 = 9; 9 + [conc.11] 2 = 11;
2 [conc.11] + 9 = 11;

2[conc.11]+2[conc.11] = 4;
4 + [conc.11] 2 = 6; 6+4 = 10;
1[conc.10] +6 = 7.

91. C.

92. 4. Add the top two digits and the middle three digits to get the total result on the bottom. Thus, 3 + 5 + 1 + [4] + 9 = 22.

93. All our dreams can come true, if we have the courage to pursue them.

94. 15. Values are as below.
● 7 ○ 2 ◉ 4

95. A=3; B=3. The logic is for the number to be 2 less than the number of intersections/overlaps.

96. 44. Add the 1st number to the 3rd number to get the 4th number, then add the 2nd to the 4th to get the 5th, 3rd to 5th to get 6th.... Thus, looking at the last 6 numbers, (13983, 20493, 30034, 44017, 64510, 945....), 13983 + 30034 = 44017; 20493 + 44017 = 64510; 30034 + 64510 = 945[44].

97. Towards the inside of the curve. The air pressure will be higher in the car at the outside of the curve than at the inside, since the air, just like the driver, has inertia and is pushed away from the curve. The balloon, filled with the lighter gas, will move to the area of lower pressure-- the inside of the curve.

98. A. The trunk is reversed.

99. There are 18 triangles. Referring to the numbered diagram below, they are: 1-2-3, 1-2-5, 1-2-7, 1-5-7, 1-7-8, 1-8-10, 2-3-5, 4-6-7, 4-6-13, 5-7-8, 6-7-9, 6-7-13, 7-8-10, 7-9-13, 7-12-13, 9-11-12, 9-12-13, and 11-12-13.

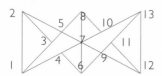

100. 15. The values are as below.
 9   ✸ 3   ✚ 2

101. 9. The values are as below.
● 3   ◆ 2   ✖ 1

102.

M	A	S	Q	U	E	R	A	D	E
O	N	T	U	N	N	I	M	O	S
V	A	A	E	B	T	D	E	W	C
E	L	I	S	I	R	I	R	N	A
M	Y	R	T	D	A	C	I	H	P
E	S	W	I	D	N	U	C	I	A
N	I	A	O	E	C	L	A	L	D
T	S	Y	N	N	E	E	N	L	E

103. 9. The sum of the top segments equals that of the bottom segments in each wheel.

104.

105.

106. H. When the numbers in both halves of each circle are added, the result should be a prime number. H (27), is the only non-prime number.

107. The dots can be joined to make 2 Roman numeral equations, shown below. The missing black dot completes the final V, at bottom right. 2 + 3 = 5; 5 - 1 = 4.

$$II + III = V$$
$$V - I = IV$$

108. The misfortunes hardest to bear are those that never come.

109. 5. In each figure the numbers add to 30.

110. The letter M.

111. A.

112. 11. The values are as below.
● 5   ○ 8   ○ 1

113. 23. The values are as below.
■ 4   ◆ 5   ▼ 6

114. The survivors made such a fuss about the prospect of being buried that the authorities decided to bury only those who didn't survive the crash.

115.

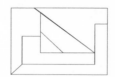

116. 62. Add the last digit of each number to the whole number to get the next number. Thus, 56 + 6 = 62.

117. LION, HYENA, TIGER, MONGOOSE, LEOPARD, FOX, WILDCAT, FERRET, CHEETAH, PANTHER.

118. An anchor.

119. A.

120. 8. The respective values are as below.
● 3   ◆ 4   ✖ 8

121. D. A represents 3 overlaps; B represents 4; C represents 5; D represents 6.

122. 8. The left and right sides of each wheel should add to the same. In C, they should add to 17.

123. None at all. Holes are already empty.

124. B & B1. There is a button missing from the second snowman from the right in B1.

125. 60.75. Each number is the result of adding half of the previous number to itself.

126. Assemble as below. E is not reqd.

127. Adding machine, Blaise Pascal; Bifocal Lens, Benjamin Franklin; Electric Light, Thomas Edison; Microphone, Alexander Graham Bell; Revolver, Samuel Colt; Vulcanised Rubber, Charles Goodyear; Jet Engine, [Sir] Frank Whittle; Chain Drive, Leonardo da Vinci.

128. 21. Values are as below.

⬜ 1 🟫 4 ⬛ 8

129. E. The indicated area has changed.

130. 8¼. Values are as below.

◆ OR ♥ = 6 OR 5
♠ = 4; ♣ = 3

131. An umbrella.

132. 12. Take the 3 smaller numbers from the top left number to get the number in the middle.

133. 13. Map the alphabet into two rows with an alphabetical offset as shown below.

12	13	1	2	3	4	5	6	7	8	9	10	11
a	b	c	d	e	f	g	h	i	j	k	l	m
n	o	p	q	r	s	t	u	v	w	x	y	z

134. A donkey.

135.

136.

137. B.

138. 21. Values are as below.

♠ 1 ♥ 4 ♣ 9

139. 121.5. Starting from the right, each successive number is the result of adding half of the previous number to itself.

140. 35. The values are as below.

🔲 3 🟫 8 🟪 9

141. YOUNG GIRLS, PARTHENOPHOBIA; WORDS, LOGOPHOBIA; TEETH, ODONTOPHOBIA; GOING TO BED, CLINOPHOBIA; STRING, LINONOPHOBIA; MONSTERS, TERATOPHOBIA; SKIN, DERMATOPHOBIA; CLOUDS, NEPHOPHOBIA.

142.

143. a. Do geese see God ?
b. The sentence is palindromic. (The letters read the same backwards.)

144.

145. 20. Values are as below.

✳ 5 ✛ 7 ⚙ 8

146. 31. This is a sequence of prime numbers. 31 is the next in the sequence.

147.

148. 107. Values are as below.

▲ 10 ● 5 ■ 3

149. a. Yes, he can take the booking.
b. As each guest arrives, he asks his existing residents to move up one room number, and he assigns room 1 to the new guest.

150. 6

151. 44. Each successive number is the result of adding the previous 3 numbers (where present).

152. 189. Reading the numbers first following (a), then (b), 765-576 = 189.

153. Success, freedom, power, harmony, health, happiness, creativity, confidence.

154. 12. The values are as below.

 I   ★ 3   ★ 5

155.

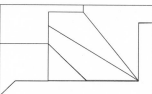

156. Maggie is not tall enough to reach the 'UP' button.

157. B.

158. B. The analogy is for the shape to reverse colors and be a mirror-image.

159. 16. 16×2=32; 32/4=8; 8×8=64; 64-4=60; 60/10=6.

160. Nondiscriminatory.

161. C & D. Totals in each pair should add to 22.

162.

163.

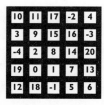

164. 3. The combined total of each circle should be 34.

165.

10	11	17	-2	4
3	9	15	16	-3
-4	2	8	14	20
19	0	1	7	13
12	18	-1	5	6

166. Better to ask the compulsive liar. That way you know it's a lie and you can then go the opposite way. With the occasional liar, you don't know whether it is the truth or not.

167.

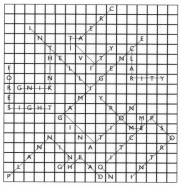

168. 6. Multiply the top two numbers together to get the bottom left and middle number, which in turn are added together to get the right bottom number. Thus 8 × 7 = 5[6]; 5 + 6=11.

169. 55. Add 1 more with every step. Thus, 2+1=3; 3+2=5; 5+3=8 .... 21+34=55.

170. Whether you think you can or cannot be successful, you will be right.

171. 15. Values are as below.

★ 2   ✳ 3   ★ 5

172. 19. 19×2=38; 38-8=30; 30/5=6; 6×6=36; 100-36=64; 64/8=8.

173. CONCOMITANT.

174. 12. Values are as below.

★ I   ★ 6   ★ 9

175.

176. M, for March. The letters represent months.

177.

3	2	9	3	1	9	5	2	5	2	1	9	3	5	1	3	2	9
9	5	2	2	9	5	3	1	1	5	3	2	9	1	3	9	5	2
5	3	1	3	1	9	5	2	2	9	5	3	1	2	9	5	3	1
9	5	2	5	2	1	9	3	3	1	9	5	2	3	1	3	9	2
2	1	5	3	9	2	1	5	1	3	9	5	2	3	9	2	1	5
3	2	9	5	1	3	2	9	3	9	2	5	1	5	1	3	2	9
5	3	1	9	2	5	3	1	5	1	3	9	2	9	2	5	3	1
9	5	2	1	3	9	5	2	9	2	5	1	3	1	3	9	5	2
1	9	3	2	5	1	9	3	1	3	9	2	5	2	5	1	9	3
2	1	5	2	9	5	3	1	2	5	1	3	9	3	9	2	1	5
3	2	9	3	1	9	5	2	5	2	1	9	3	5	1	3	2	9
5	3	1	5	2	1	9	3	9	3	2	1	5	9	2	5	3	1
9	5	2	2	9	5	3	1	1	5	3	2	9	1	3	9	5	2
5	3	1	3	1	9	5	2	2	9	5	3	1	2	9	5	3	1
9	5	2	5	2	1	9	3	3	1	9	5	2	3	1	3	9	2
1	9	3	1	3	9	5	2	5	2	5	2	1	9	3	1	9	3

178. A mountain. (White fruit: snow analogy)

179. TT, for Twenty-three. The letters represent numbers.

180. C.

PUZZLE 1

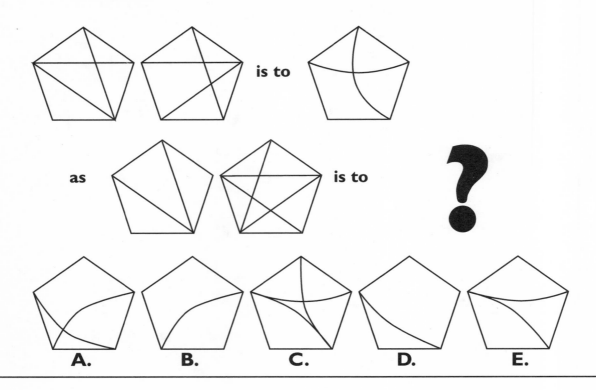

is to

as

is to

?

A.   B.   C.   D.   E.

PUZZLE 2

Take a word from each column in turn to find four compound words.
For example: the five words 'door, step, child, birth, mark' would produce the words 'doorstep, stepchild, childbirth, birthmark'.

A	B	C	D	E
make	key	less	smith	boy
pin	some	or	on	set
turn	cross	time	play	top
dove	tail	word	bit	cost
wag	shift	body	table	land

LEVEL 2

PUZZLE 3

In this grid the word 'banana' written without a change of direction appears ony once. It can be written forwards and backwards in a horizontal, vertical or diagonal. Can you spot it?

```
B A B A N A N B A N B N A N B A
N N N A B A A A B A N N A A N
A N A B N N B A N B A N N A
N A B B A N N A N A B A B N B
A N A N B A A A N A B A B A A
B A N A B N A B A A N A A N A N
A B A A B A N A A B A N B A N A
N A A B A N A N B A N B A B A B
A N A N B N B N A B A A N A N A
B A N A A N A A B A A N A N N N
N B B N N N A N A N A N B A N A
A A N A A B A A N N A A B B A B
B N A B A N A B A B N A N A N A
A B N A B A N B A B N A N B A N
N A A B A N A A A A N B A B N A
A N A N B A B N B A N A N B A N
```

PUZZLE 4

When this pattern is folded to form a cube, just one of the following can be produced. Which one?

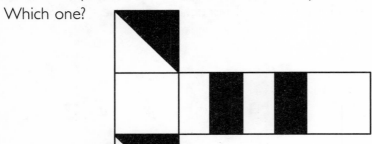

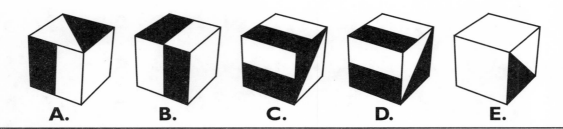

A.   **B.**   **C.**   **D.**   **E.**

PUZZLE 5

Take one letter from each of the clouds in order. You will be able to make the names of six boys and girls who are also saints.

1. C H U M A T

2. E A N H L R

3. D R A S L O

4. M R U I T E

5. L R I E N A

6. E A S N A W

PUZZLE 6

Which is the odd one out?

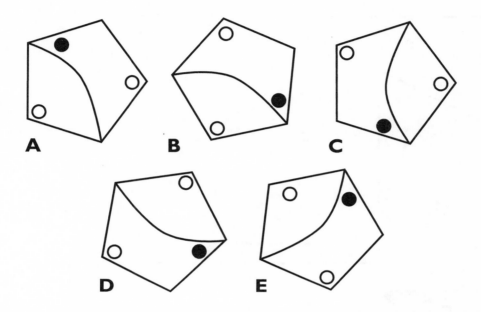

PUZZLE 7

Which pair of letters comes next in this sequence?

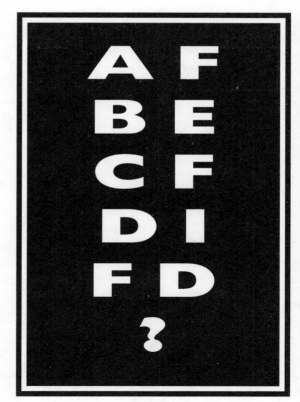

PUZZLE 8

Fit the seven pieces together to construct a letter of the alphabet.

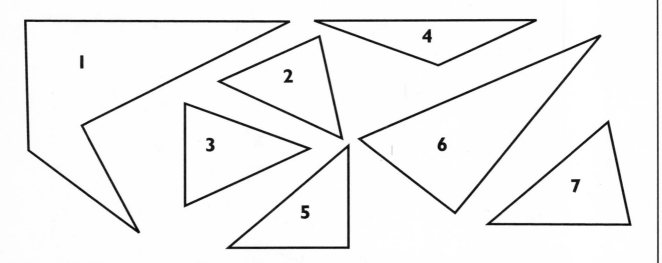

PUZZLE 9

Which pentagon is missing from the top of the pyramid?

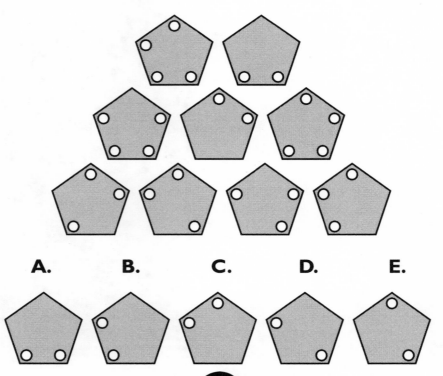

A.   B.   C.   D.   E.

PUZZLE 10

Unscramble these five anagrammed words to determine their commonality or relationship.

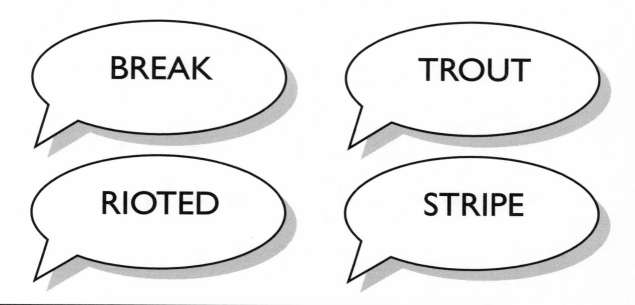

BREAK

TROUT

RIOTED

STRIPE

PUZZLE 11

Which is the odd one out?

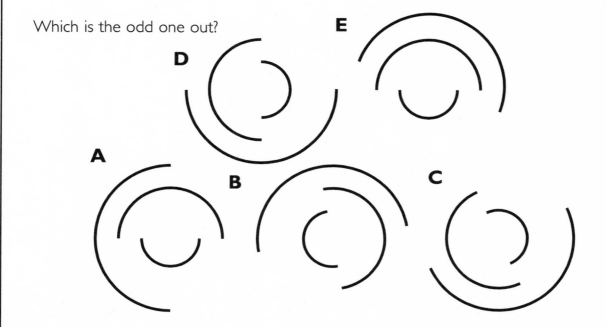

PUZZLE 12

Which set completes the above?

PUZZLE 13

Which is the missing section?

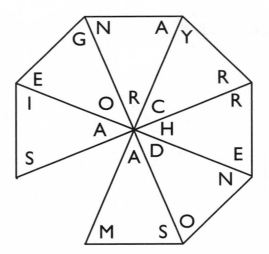

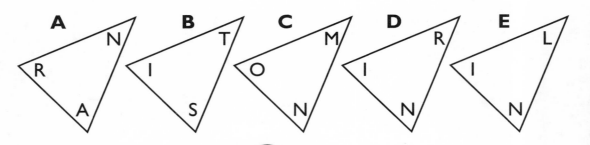

PUZZLE 14

To which number should the missing hand be pointing on the last clock face?

PUZZLE 15

Which is the odd one out?

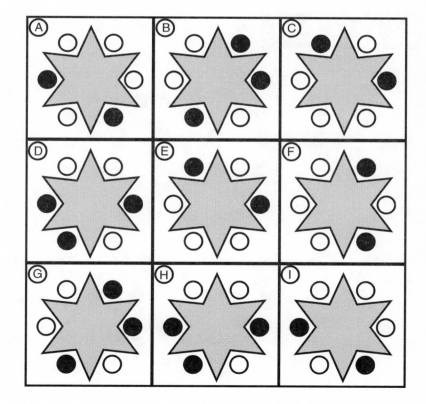

PUZZLE 16

What letter is missing from this diagram?

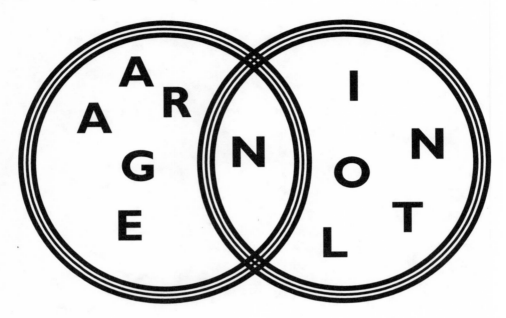

PUZZLE 17

Which die below continues the above sequence?

A.　　　**B.**　　　**C.**　　　**D.**　　　**E.**

PUZZLE 18

Which pair of letters are the odd one out?

EV LO KP BY DW HS GT JR

PUZZLE 19

Which is the missing box?

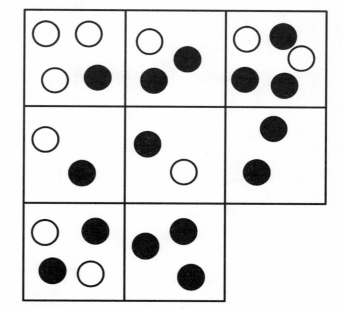

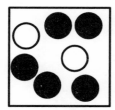

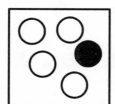

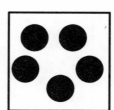

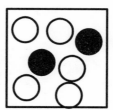

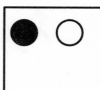

A.   **B.**   **C.**   **D.**   **E.**

PUZZLE 20

Which number should replace the question mark?

			44				42			
						74				
	29									
16						63				
12		23				33				
				63				31		
			52			?				
						83				
		42			24					
	38									

PUZZLE 21

Which letter does not belong in the circle?

PUZZLE 22

Take one letter from each word in turn working downwards to spell out an American city. Then do the same again, this time using different letters to spell out another American city, then do the same again to spell out a third American city.

E	M	E	N	D	A	T	E
D	O	N	A	T	I	O	N
B	L	U	E	C	A	P	S
H	E	A	R	T	I	L	Y
H	A	L	L	M	A	R	K
S	A	U	C	I	E	S	T

PUZZLE 23

Pick a letter from each cloud to find six weather related words. All letters are in the order of clouds shown except one of the words where the order is all mixed up.

1. D N T T C R

2. O D Y R A Y

3. I C O R H P

4. U N U L N H

5. E G B O A O

6. O N H O T D

7. O W T N R E

PUZZLE 24

Which option below is missing in this array?

    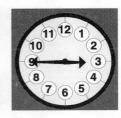

A.   **B.**   **C.**   **D.**   **E.**

PUZZLE 25

Create two words using the following 10 letters once each.

Clue: Personal attraction.

NTEGOMYDBA

PUZZLE 26

Which piece below can be fitted to the piece above to form a perfect circle?

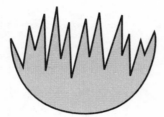

A.   **B.**   **C.**   **D.**   **E.**

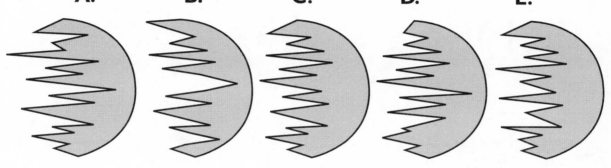

PUZZLE 27

The code reveals a book title and author. Can you crack it?

119
198
251
1511
215
1219
916
115
51
918
205

PUZZLE 28

What month comes next?

JANUARY OCTOBER
MARCH   MARCH
JUNE   ?

PUZZLE 29

What letter should replace the question mark?

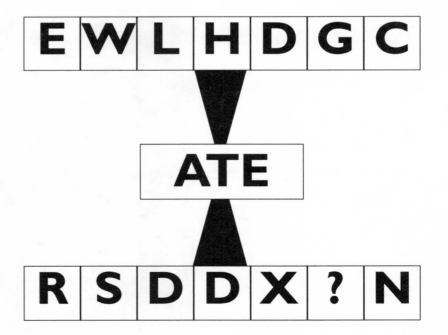

E W L H D G C

ATE

R S D D X ? N

PUZZLE 30

Which is the odd one out?

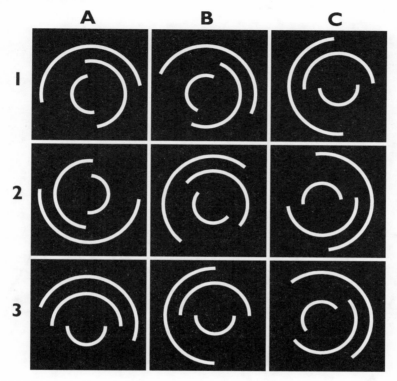

A   B   C

1

2

3

PUZZLE 31

What numbers should appear on the bottom row?

12	18	27	14
41	39	32	30
62	73	69	80
?	?	?	?

PUZZLE 32

Which triangle below is missing from the top of the pyramid?

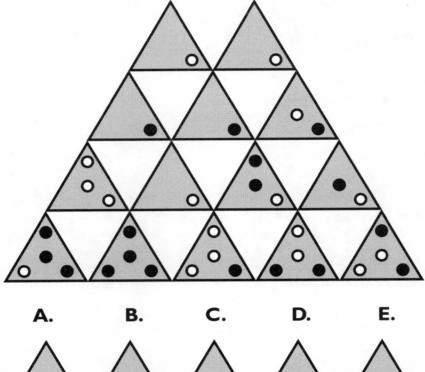

A. B. C. D. E.

PUZZLE 33

Paul visited five American states

HE HATED KENTUCKY
HE LOVED INDIANA
HE LOVED NORTH CAROLINA
HE HATED LOUISIANA

Did he love or hate Maryland?

PUZZLE 34

To what number should the missing arrow point on the fourth clock face?

PUZZLE 35

Which is the odd one out?

A.

B.

C.

D.

E.

PUZZLE 36

Which day is two days before the day after the day three days after the day before Tuesday?

| SUNDAY |
| MONDAY |
| TUESDAY |
| WEDNESDAY |
| THURSDAY |
| FRIDAY |
| SATURDAY |

PUZZLE 37

What continues the sequence?

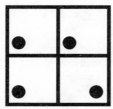 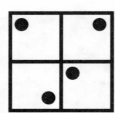 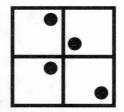

A.   **B.**   **C.**   **D.**   **E.**

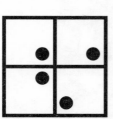 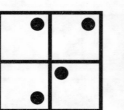 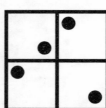 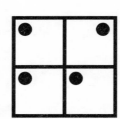 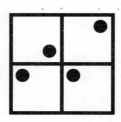

PUZZLE 38

The letters missing from this list can be arranged into a significant event. Three of the missing letters appear twice.

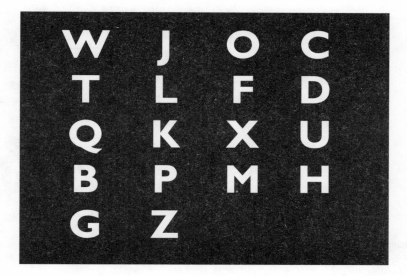

W J O C
T L F D
Q K X U
B P M H
G Z

PUZZLE 39

Which is the odd one out?

A.   B.   C.   D.   E.

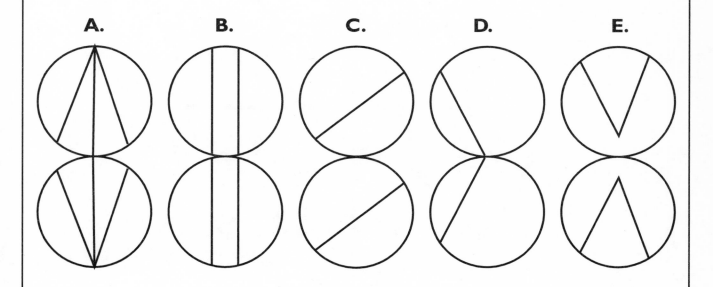

PUZZLE 40

Make PIE   HUMBLE   by following these instruction:

1. Change a letter

2. Change a letter

3. Change a letter

4. Add three letters

HUMBLE

PUZZLE 41

What number should replace the question mark?

PUZZLE 42

Which is the odd one out?

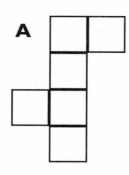

A

B

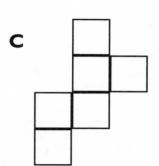

C

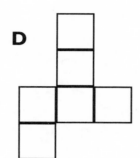

D

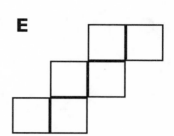

E

PUZZLE 43

What number should replace the question mark?

456	128	37
648	548	96
263	?	89

PUZZLE 44

In the grid the word 'Ohio', written without a change of direction, appears only once. It can be written forwards and backwards in a horizontal, vertical or diagonal direction. Can you spot it?

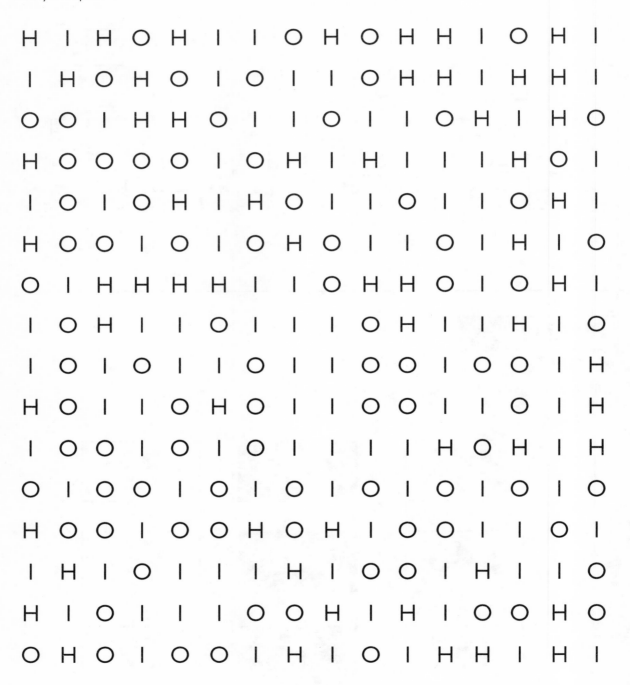

```
H I H O H I I O H O H H I O H I
I H O H O I O I I O H H I H H I
O O I H H O I I O I I O H I H O
H O O O O I O H I H I I I H O I
I O I O H I H O I I O I I O H I
H O O I O I O H O I I O I H I O
O I H H H H I I O H H O I O H I
I O H I I O I I I O H I I H I O
I O I O I I O I I O O I O O I H
H O I I O H O I I O O I I O I H
I O O I O I O I I I I H O H I H
O I O O I O I O I O I O I O I O
H O O I O O H O H I O O I I O I
I H I O I I I H I O O I H I I O
H I O I I I O O H I H I O O H O
O H O I O O I H I O I H H I H I
```

LEVEL 2

PUZZLE 45

When this pattern is folded to form a cube, just one of the following can be produced. Which one?

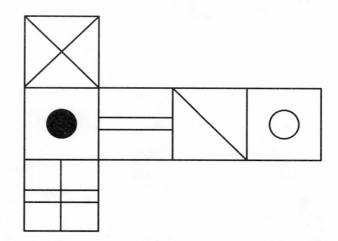

A. 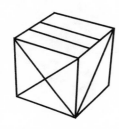 **B.** 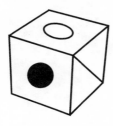 **C.**  **D.** 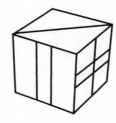 **E.**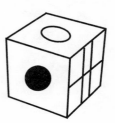

PUZZLE 46

Which is the odd one out?

A 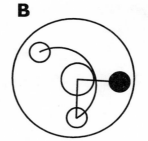 B

C 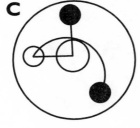 D 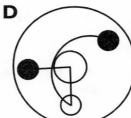 E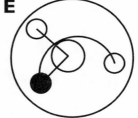

F 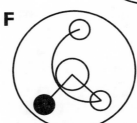 G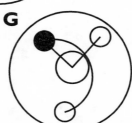

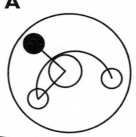

LEVEL 2

PUZZLE 47

Take one letter from each bottle in order to find 5 insects.

PUZZLE 48

Which dice face should replace the question mark?

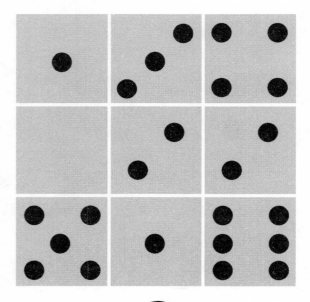

128

PUZZLE 49

This is a treasure map. The treasure is marked T. You have to start by finding the commencing square.

N

3S	IW	3S	IW
3E	IN	T	IS
IN	IW	IN	IW
3E	IN	IW	3N

W   **E**

3S means move 3 squares south. Every square is visited.

S

PUZZLE 50

Take one letter from each container in order and find 5 trees.

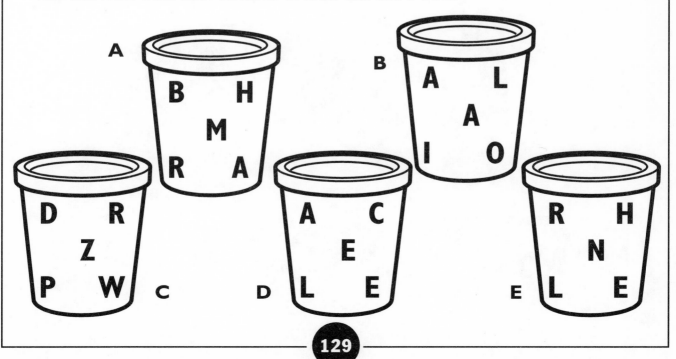

PUZZLE 51

Each of the nine squares in the grid marked 1A to 3C, should incorporate all the lines and symbols which are shown in the squares of the same letter and number immediately above and to the left. For example, 2B should incorporate all the lines and symbols that are in 2 and B.
One of the squares in incorrect. Which one is it?

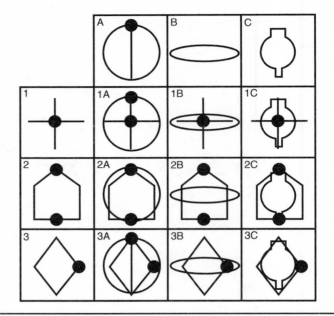

PUZZLE 52

Can you find the position of the bottle to replace the question mark?

PUZZLE 53

How many circles are there?

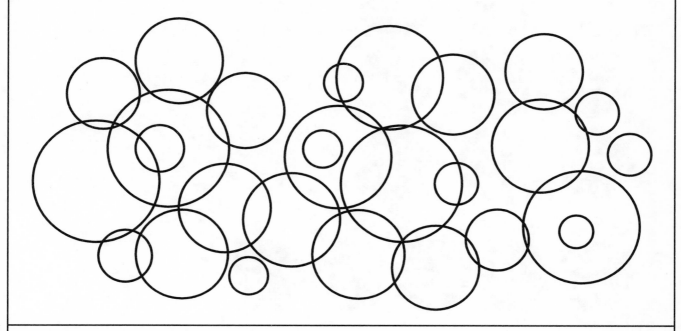

PUZZLE 54

The numbers in the square follow a pattern. Can you unravel it and change the question mark for a number?

12	4	8	6
6	4	5	15
2	5	17	?
4	13	4	2

PUZZLE 55

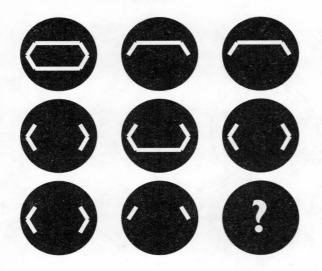

Which circle should replace the question mark?

PUZZLE 56

What number should replace the question mark to a definite rule?

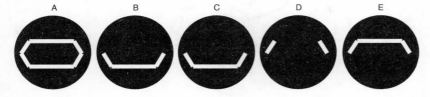

34	31	33	32
30	35	29	36
38	27	37	28
26	39	25	?

START

PUZZLE 57

What number should replace the question mark to a definite rule?

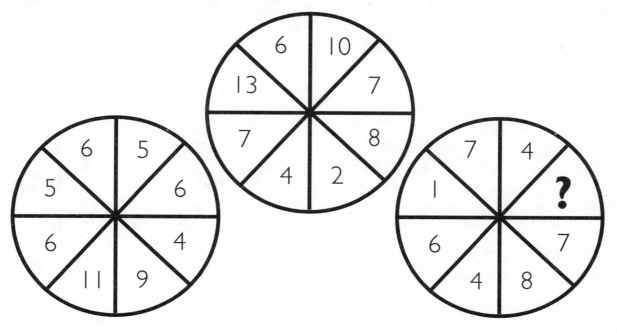

PUZZLE 58

There is a system for pricing the menu, what would oysters cost?

Menu

Soup	$10
Salad	$14
Roast Beef	$24
Ice Cream	$20
Coffee	$15

PUZZLE 59

Each line and symbol which appears in the four outer circles is transferred to the center circle according to these rules:

If a line or symbol occurs in the outer circles:
once:..it is transferred
twice:........................it is possibly transferred
3 times:......................................it is transferred
4 times:............................it is not transferred

Which of the circles A, B, C, D or E, should appear at the center of the diagram?

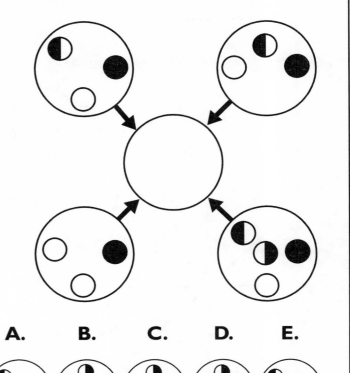

A. **B.** **C.** **D.** **E.**

PUZZLE 60

What number should replace the question mark?

PUZZLE 61

Place the letters in the grid to make a fish and a flower.

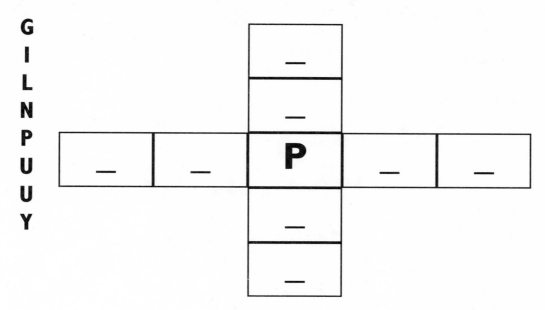

PUZZLE 62

Place 3 two-letter bits together to form a drink.

AP CO FF
RI PA GR

PUZZLE 63

Each pair of circles produces the circle above by carrying forward only those elements that are different. Similar elements are cancelled out.

Find the circle to replace the question mark.

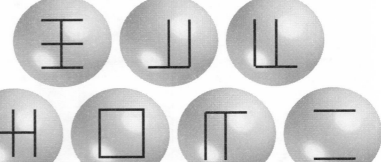

A.   B.   C.   D.   E.

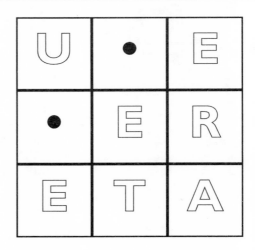

PUZZLE 64

Fill in the missing letters to make a 9-letter word. Starting from a corner square and spiral in to the center.

U	•	E
•	E	R
E	T	A

PUZZLE 65

Fill in the blank spaces to find two words which are synonyms.

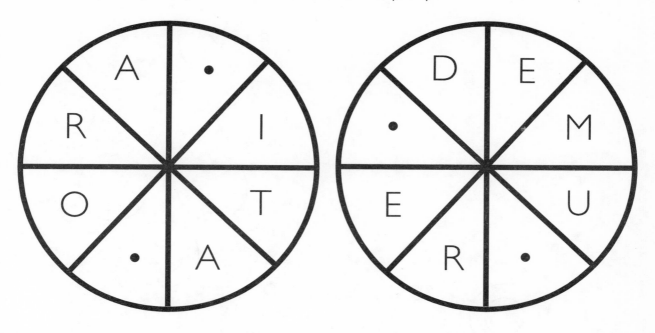

PUZZLE 66

Fill in the missing letters to find an 8-letter word.

PUZZLE 67

Which circle should replace the question mark?

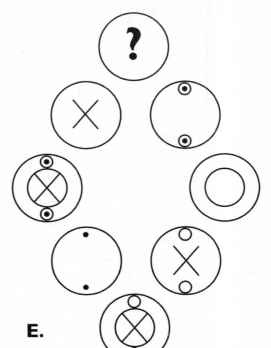

A.   **B.**   **C.**   **D.**   **E.**

PUZZLE 68

What number should replace the question mark?

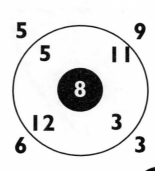

PUZZLE 69

Fill in the missing letters to find food on the menu.

	A		S		R		L	
	R		C		S		E	
	I		C		M		A	
	C		N		T		E	
	P		G		E		T	
	A		B		R		E	

PUZZLE 70

How many triangles are there in this diagram?

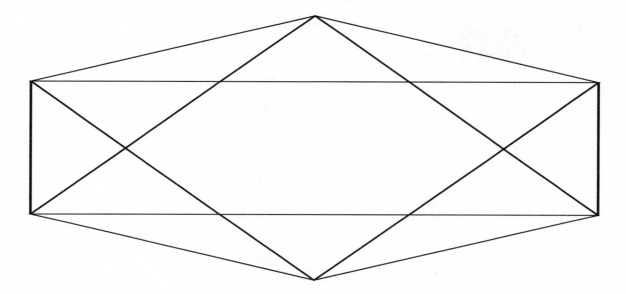

PUZZLE 71

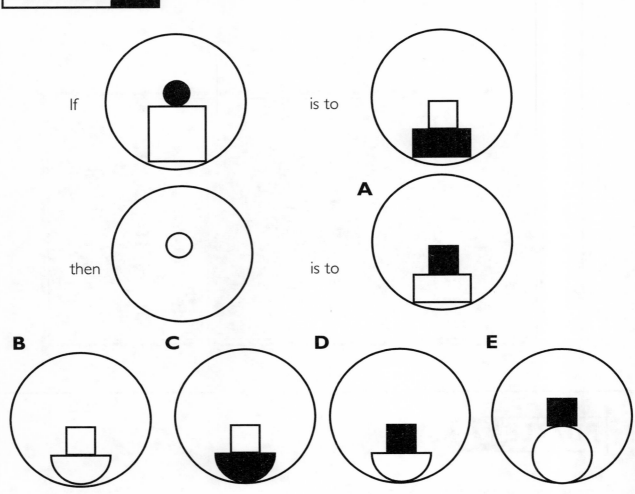

If [ ] is to A

then [ ] is to

B   C   D   E

PUZZLE 72

Which word will fit in front of these words to form new words?

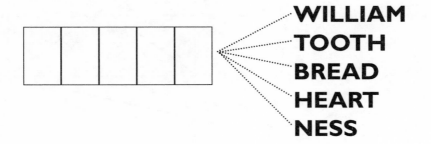

WILLIAM
TOOTH
BREAD
HEART
NESS

PUZZLE 73

What number should replace the question mark?

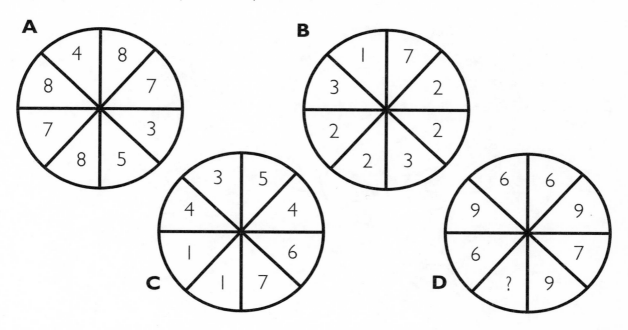

A

B

C

D

PUZZLE 74

What number should replace the question mark?

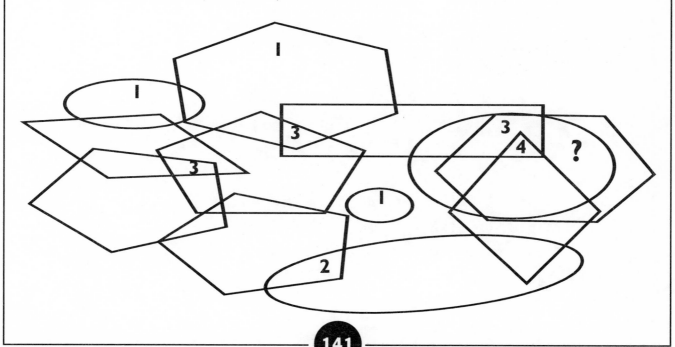

PUZZLE 75

Rearrange the letters to form each set into a flower.

PUZZLE 76

Mr Smith went on vacation to America

He liked New York
But not Maine
He liked Colorado
But not Wisconsin
He liked Nevada
But not Chicago
He liked Dallas
But not Michigan

Did he like Idaho?

PUZZLE 77

Multiply the largest prime number by the smallest even number.

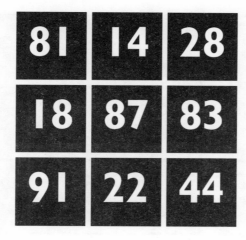

81	14	28
18	87	83
91	22	44

PUZZLE 78

How many squares are there in this diagram?

PUZZLE 79

Start at a corner square move along a spiral route and find the rule for the numbering and replace the question mark.

34	30	36	32
28	44	40	38
32	38	?	34
26	42	36	40

PUZZLE 80

Find the names of biblical characters by filling in the blanks.

```
_ A _     _ L
_ P _     _ R     _ I _
_ A _     _ O     _
_ H _     _ D     _ A     _ H
_ E _     _ J     _ M     _ N
_ A _     _ H     _ H     _ B _
_ E _     _ O     _
_ B _     _ A     _ A     _
_ O _     _ E     _
_ O _     _ E     _ H
```

PUZZLE 81

A fish farmer had to visit his 10 lakes every day. Each visit to a lake meant a return journey to his house before the next lake visit.

Where should he build his house for the least amount of travelling?

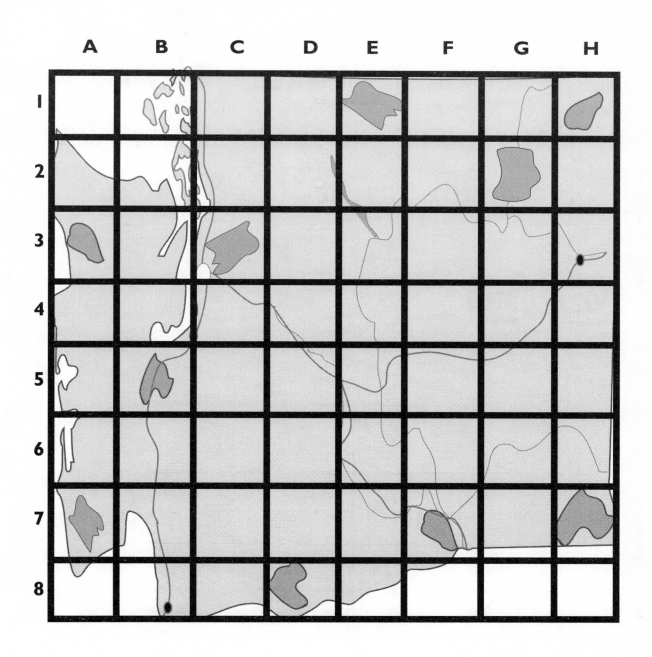

PUZZLE 82

Find 5 animals in these sentences.

1. Give the imp a large brandy.

2. Have a holiday on a German lake.

3. Watch out for he suspects you.

4. Place the saucepan the right way up.

5. Make sure that it's level and true.

PUZZLE 83

Find a 3-letter word which, when placed on the end of these words, makes new words.

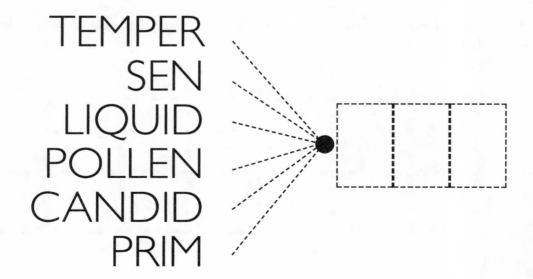

TEMPER
SEN
LIQUID
POLLEN
CANDID
PRIM

PUZZLE 84

What number should replace the question mark?

11 2 9¾ 5½ 8½ 9 7¼ ?

PUZZLE 85

How many revolutions are made by a 28-inch bicycle wheel over one mile?

PUZZLE 86

Which of these words in B could fit into A for a definite reason?

CLASPING
PAPERS
SEWED
SKIDDED
TOXIC
?

A

BROOM
DISMAL
SCUBA
CHANGE
BELONG

B

PUZZLE 87

Each line and symbol which appears in the four outer circles is transferred to the center circle according to these rules:

If a line or symbol occurs in the outer circles:
once: it is transferred
twice: it is possibly transferred
3 times: it is transferred
4 times: it is not transferred.

Which of the circles A, B, C, D or E, shown below should appear at the center of the diagram,?

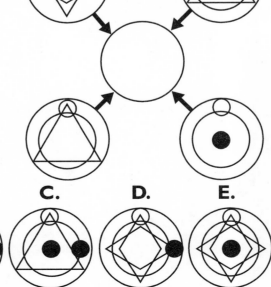

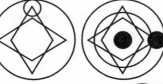

A.   **B.**   **C.**   **D.**   **E.**

PUZZLE 88

One man can paint a fence in 2 hours
One man can paint a fence in 3 hours
One man can paint a fence in 4 hours
One man can paint a fence in 6 hours

If they all worked together on the fence, each working at his same speed as before, how long would it take?

PUZZLE 89

Arrange these 12 objects into 4 sets of three.

LAMPREY   TARSUS   SAFFRON

CLARET   HERRING   ANISEED

SCAPULA   ANCHOVY   HEMLOCK

CYPRESS   SORREL   FIBULA

PUZZLE 90

Which is the odd one out?

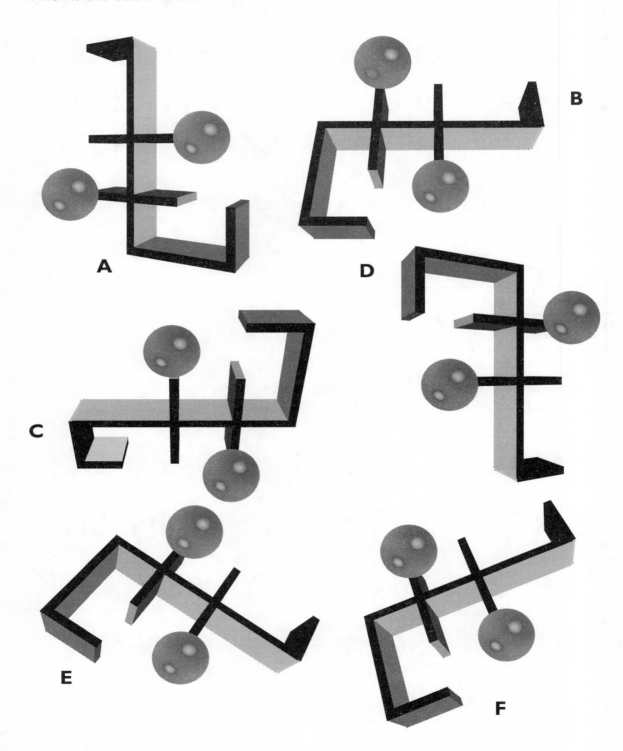

PUZZLE 91

What number should replace the question mark?

PUZZLE 92

Which of the following cannot be made from this layout?

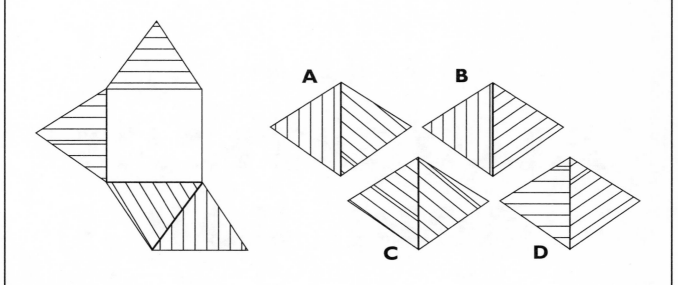

PUZZLE 93

Which figure is the odd one out?

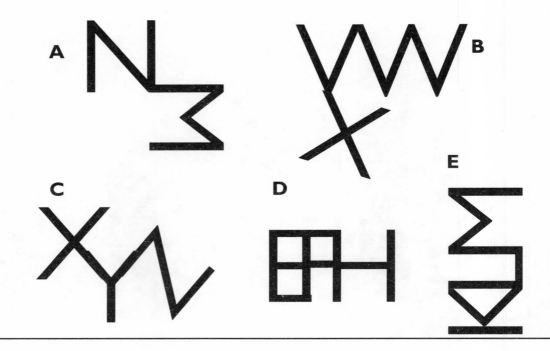

PUZZLE 94

Arrange all of the letters of the newspaper headline below to spell out three musical instruments.

NICE ALLOCATIONS ROBS COP

PUZZLE 95

Ken dropped a sugar cube into his coffee, then lifted it out 2 minutes later intact.
How was he able to do this?

PUZZLE 96

  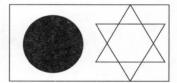

What comes next in this sequence?

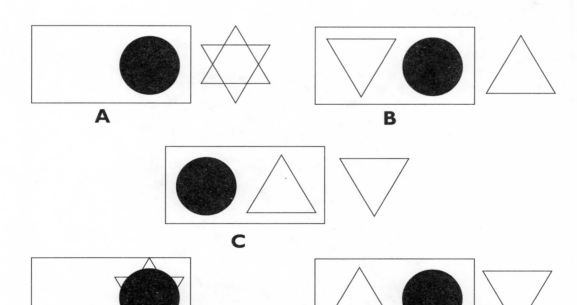

A

B

C

D

E

PUZZLE 97

What number should replace the question mark?

16	8	6
20	3	6
9	3	?

PUZZLE 98

What number continues this sequence?

1921
1315
2021
235
?

PUZZLE 99

Which of the five boxes below is most like the box at right?

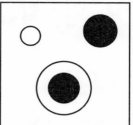

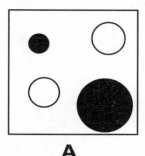

A

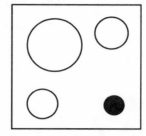

B

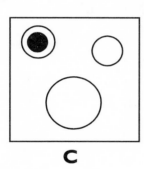

C

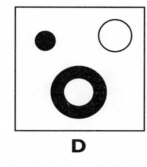

D

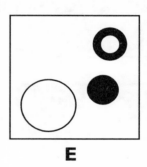

E

PUZZLE 100

An American citizen with no passport visits 10 foreign countries in one day. He is welcomed in each country and leaves of his own accord.
How is he able to do this?

PUZZLE 101

What word is coded to appear in the middle box?

| DYNAMIC | ADORN | PROFUSE |

| RETORTS | ? | LIBERTY |

PUZZLE 102

Which number is the odd one out?

364 299
693
562
484
364
772 136

PUZZLE 103

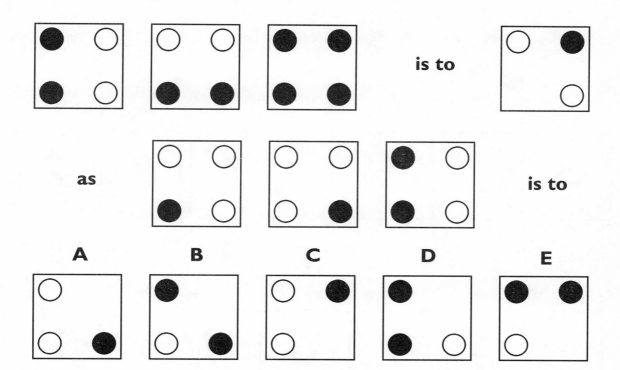

is to

as

is to

| A | B | C | D | E |

PUZZLE 104

Take one letter from each shield in turn to spell out five types of fabric. The six letters left over can be arranged into another type of fabric.

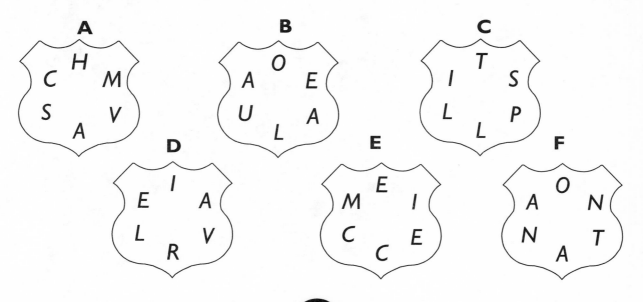

LEVEL 2

PUZZLE 105

Which number should replace the question mark?

```
    2              5
3   7   6      7   8   2

    ?
    7   6   4
```

PUZZLE 106

Which is the odd one out?

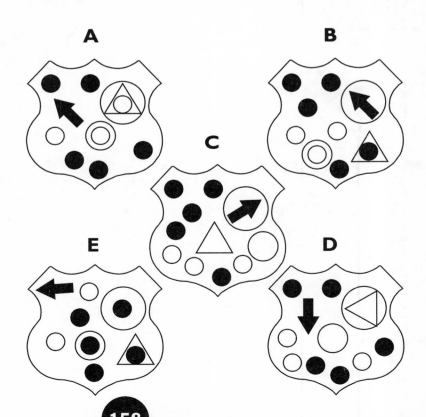

A   B   C   E   D

158

PUZZLE 107

Which piece below when fitted to the above piece will form a perfect square?

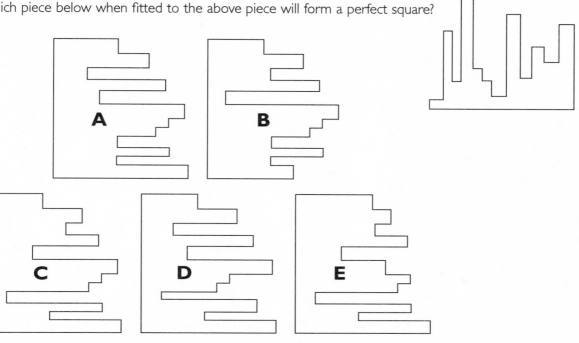

PUZZLE 108

What number should replace the question mark?

PUZZLE 109

A man walked into an inn and asked for a glass of water. The innkeeper produced a gun and shot it into the air. Shortly afterwards the man thanked him and walked out.
Why?

PUZZLE 110

What letter should replace the question mark?

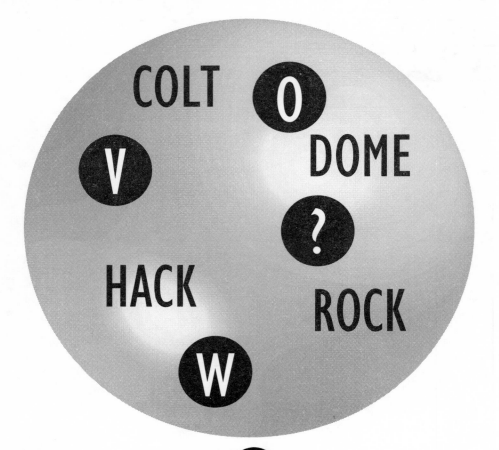

PUZZLE 111

What comes next in this sequence?

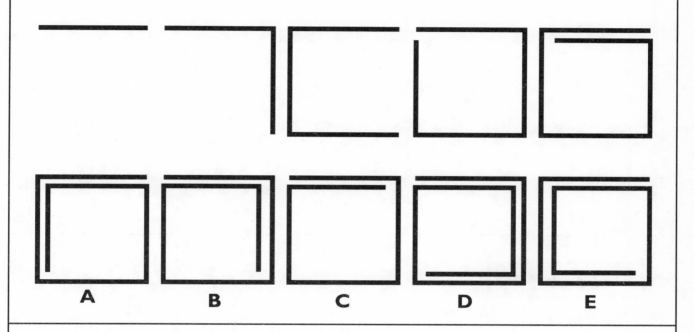

A   B   C   D   E

PUZZLE 112

Replace the question mark with the four main mathematical signs, two of them twice, to complete the equation.

PUZZLE 113

In this anagram puzzle you are looking for a foodstuff, however, only the letters which you do not need to complete the puzzle are shown.

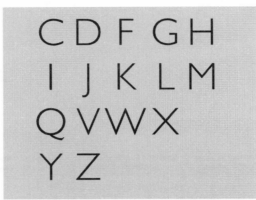

C D F G H
I J K L M
Q V W X
Y Z

PUZZLE 114

What should replace the question mark?

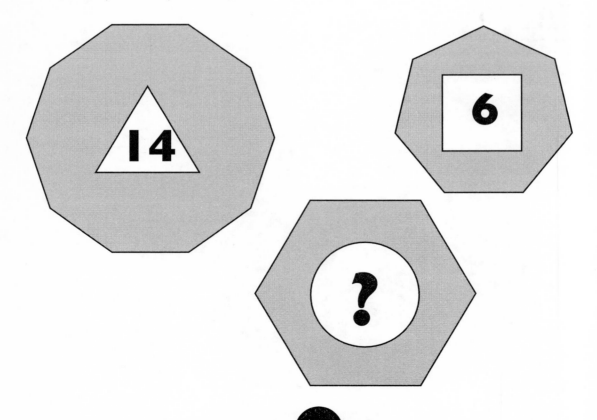

14

6

?

LEVEL 2

PUZZLE 115

What number should replace the question mark?

PUZZLE 116

What letter should replace the question mark?

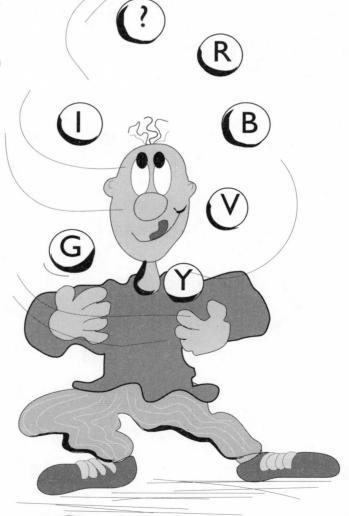

PUZZLE 117

What should replace the question mark?

9	14
J	O
16	?

PUZZLE 118

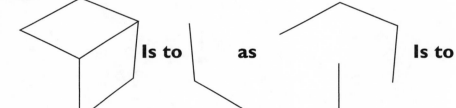

Is to   as   Is to

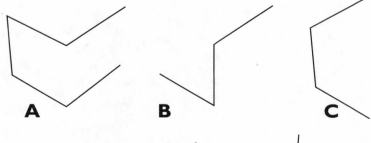

A   B   C

D   E

PUZZLE 119

What should replace the question mark?

PUZZLE 120

Which of the boxes has a property similar to the example below?

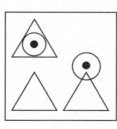

A

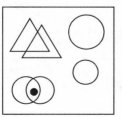

B

C

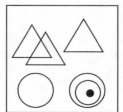

D

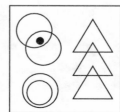

E

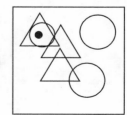

PUZZLE 121

In this grid the word 'TIPTOE', written without a change of direction appears only once. It can be written forwards or backwards in a horizontal, vertical or diagonal direction. Can you spot it?

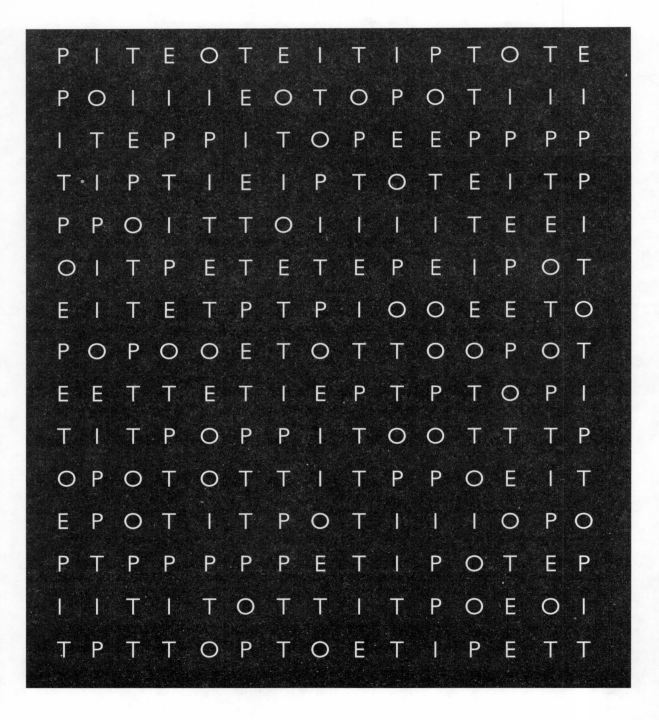

```
P I T E O T E I T I P T O T E
P O I I I E O T O P O T I I I
I T E P P I T O P E E P P P
T I P T I E I P T O T E I T P
P P O I T T O I I I I T E E I
O I T P E T E T E P E I P O T
E I T E T P T P I O O E E T O
P O P O O E T O T T O O P O T
E E T T E T I E P T P T O P I
T I T P O P P I T O O T T P
O P O T O T T I T P P O E I T
E P O T I T P O T I I I O P O
P T P P P P E T I P O T E P
I I T I T T O T T I T P O E O I
T P T T O P T O E T I P E T T
```

PUZZLE 122

Move 6 matchsticks to form 3 squares and 1 triangle.

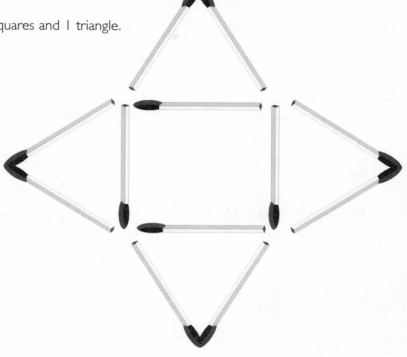

PUZZLE 123

What number should replace the question mark?

PUZZLE 124

Which word in the right-hand list should be transferred to the left-hand list?

DEMURE
AMULET
MORATORIUM
MULTIGERM

TURNKEY
BREWERY
EMERGENCY
CRESCENT
PORTRAIT

PUZZLE 125

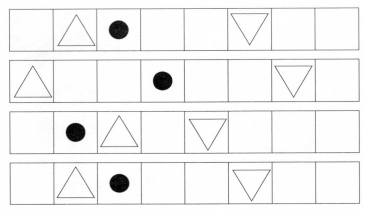

What comes next in the above sequence?

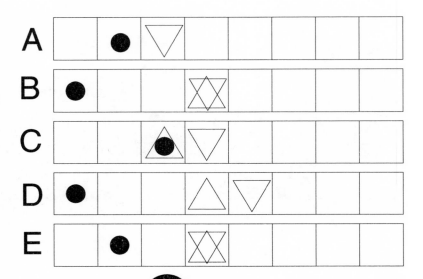

PUZZLE 126

Create two words using the following 10 letters once each only.

Clue: Macabre mountain.

PUZZLE 127

Brian died in Texas, while Cathy died at sea. Cathy's death was a cause for much celebration, after Brian. **Why?**

PUZZLE 128

Unscramble these four anagrammed words to determine their commonality or relationship.

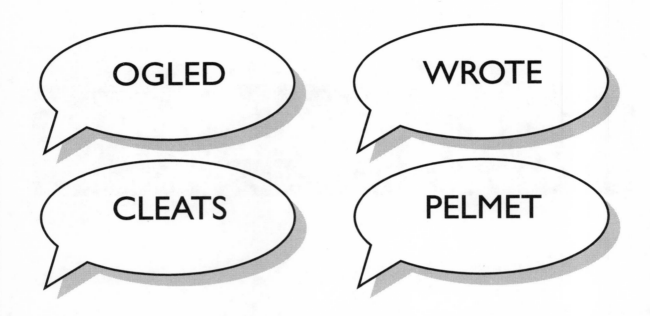

OGLED

WROTE

CLEATS

PELMET

PUZZLE 129

What number in the grid is 3 places away from itself doubled, four places away from itself plus 2, 5 places away from itself plus 6, and two places away from itself times 4?

14	36	63	62	25	52	12	41	81
70	57	6	33	2	53	31	15	56
42	22	64	45	19	73	7	46	27
29	76	18	10	78	40	16	61	3
71	17	77	44	34	69	23	37	51
49	26	54	79	4	24	60	43	8
58	11	9	65	35	55	5	21	32
30	80	1	47	59	28	66	13	68
72	38	39	75	20	74	50	48	67

PUZZLE 130

What word is coded to appear in the central rectangle?

BUNDLE   DAMSEL   MOSAIC

SCREEN   ?   GUINEA

PUZZLE 131

What letter is two to the left of the letter immediately to the left of the letter four to the right of the letter three to the left of the letter 'D'?

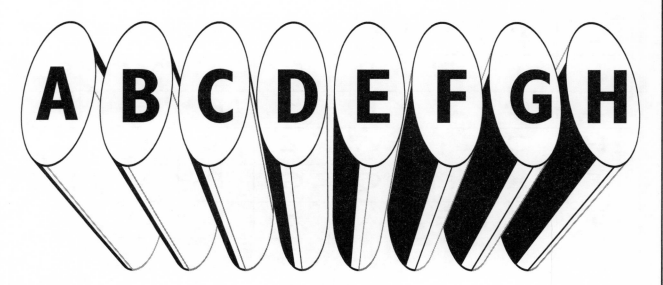

A B C D E F G H

PUZZLE 132

What number replaces the question mark?

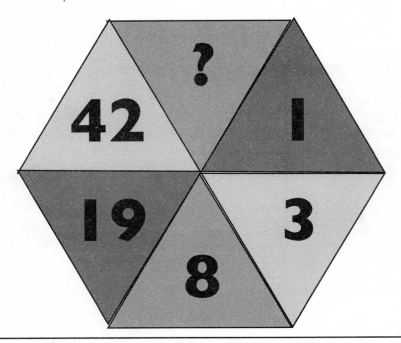

PUZZLE 133

Delete the letters that appear more thatn once and rearrange the remaining letters to spell out the name of a city.

L	V	C	G	T	Y	Q	J
F	I	U	P	G	A	W	F
Z	C	Y	R	K	E	H	S
H	O	J	W	Z	N	B	L
F	X	M	Q	G	P	V	U
T	B	E	K	X	R	D	C

PUZZLE 134

A man walked into a clothes store wearing some old tattered jeans and took a new pair into the changing room to try on. Five minutes later he left the store wearing the new jeans without paying for them and left his old tattered jeans in the changing room. No one saw him commit the act nor was he caught on security camera, yet when he arrived home the police were waiting for him.

How did they know?

PUZZLE 135

What number should replace the question mark?

6	1	2	3	6
5	3	9	1	5
6	1	?	3	6
2	6	6	4	2
5	2	1	4	5

PUZZLE 136

Each of the nine squares in the grid marked 1A to 3C, should incorporate all the lines and symbols which are shown in the squares of the same letter and number immediately above and to the left. For example, 2B should incorporate all the lines and symbols that are in 2 and B. One of the squares is incorrect. Which one is it?

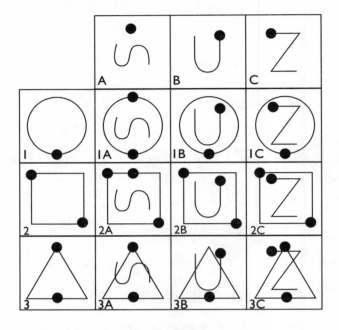

PUZZLE 137

Where is each balloon heading – find the city to replace the question mark.

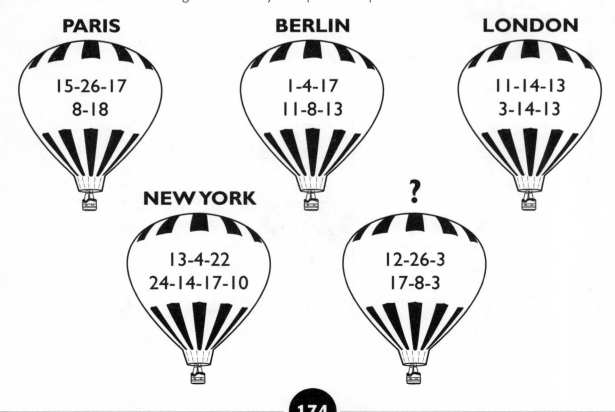

PARIS
15-26-17
8-18

BERLIN
1-4-17
11-8-13

LONDON
11-14-13
3-14-13

NEW YORK
13-4-22
24-14-17-10

?
12-26-3
17-8-3

PUZZLE 138

Which symbol should replace the question mark?

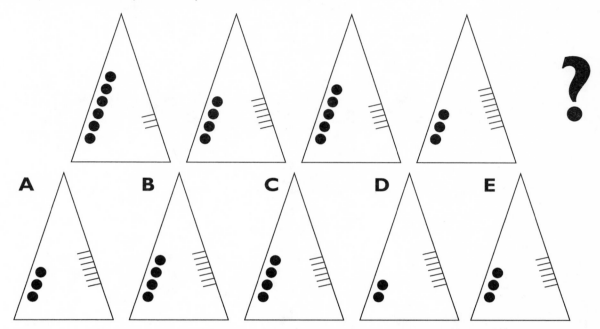

A   B   C   D   E

PUZZLE 139

Take a letter from each in order and find 6 electrical terms.

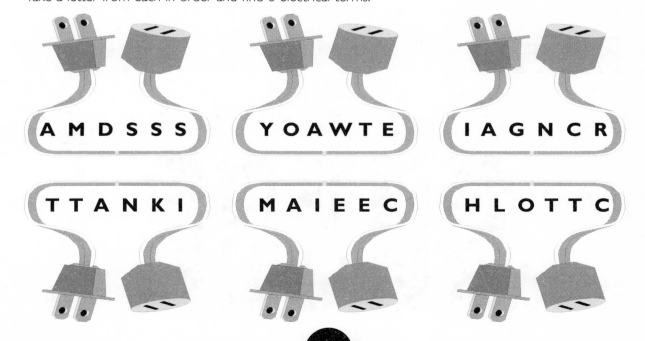

A M D S S S   Y O A W T E   I A G N C R

T T A N K I   M A I E E C   H L O T T C

PUZZLE 140

Which symbols should replace the question mark, A, B, C, D or E?

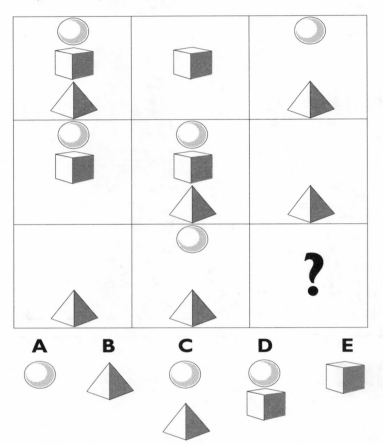

PUZZLE 141

Can you unravel the logic behind these domino pieces and fill in the missing letter.

PUZZLE 142

The missing letters rearranged will show you my answer.

J D P G O U
Z V I C B H
L K F X T Q

PUZZLE 143

Which circle should replace the question mark?

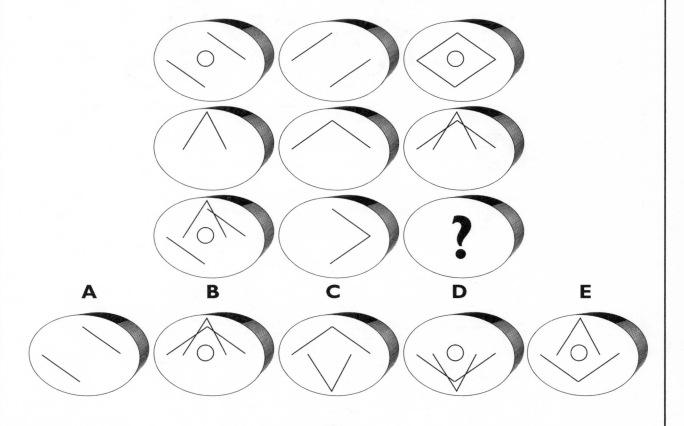

A   B   C   D   E

PUZZLE 144

Can you work out the connection between the units of fuel purchased and the number plate and find out how many units were purchased by T529CTM ?

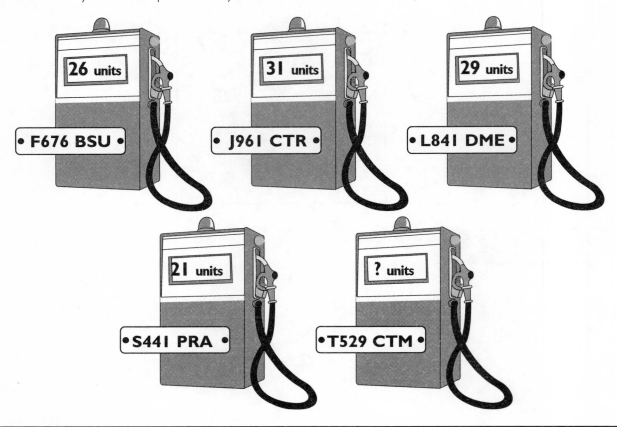

PUZZLE 145

Unravel the reasoning behind this diagram to find the number to replace the question mark.

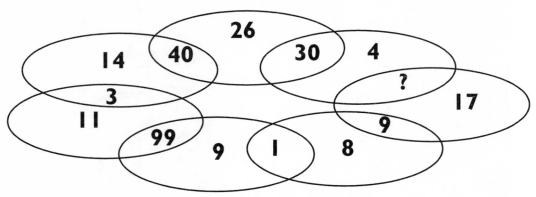

PUZZLE 146

Which figure completes the sequence?

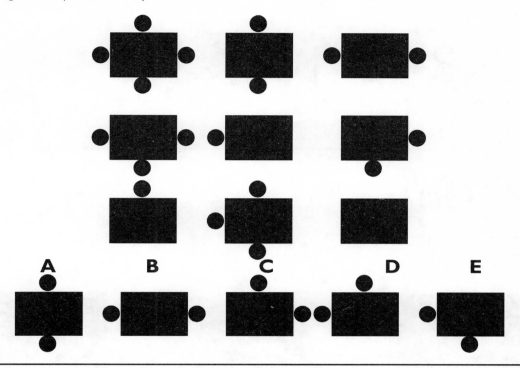

PUZZLE 147

Which is the odd number out in each circle?

1331   9   13   15   729   11   2197

8   16   64   144   18   12   256

PUZZLE 148

Can you find the next number in this sequence?

2 3 6 10 17 28 46 ?

PUZZLE 149

Which is the odd shape?

PUZZLE 150

Which symbol should replace the question mark?

KⲄOⱵVX
LOTⴸXⱯ
OⱵVXAƎ
TⴸXⱯƎ?
VXAEFC

KⲄOⱵVXLⴸTAEFCⱵ

PUZZLE 151

Which figure completes the sequence, A, B, C or D?

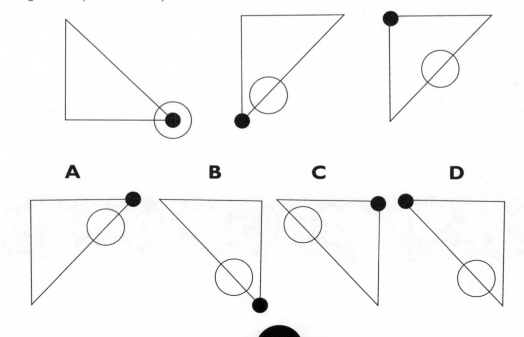

A　　**B**　　**C**　　**D**

PUZZLE 152

Which word in B could be placed in A to match up with the other words?

A

AUTOMOTIVE

CAULIFLOWER

ACCENTUATION

DIALOGUE

GREGARIOUS

B

REASONING

COMBINATION

CAUTIONED

INTELLIGENCE

HORIZONTAL

PUZZLE 153

Find a reason for arranging these numbers into 3 groups of three.

127 245 371 453 580 596 619 864 967

PUZZLE 154

Fill in the missing numbers.

6	3	4	7	5	8
8	7	5	8	2	6
3	6		1	4	8
4	8	5	8	7	
7	2		7		3
5	6	8	4	7	6

PUZZLE 155

Which of the figures completes the sequence A, B, C or D?

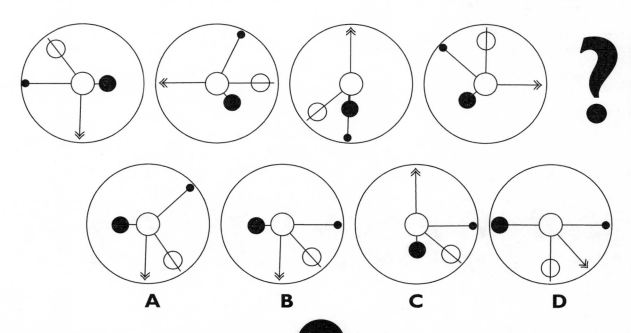

A   B   C   D

PUZZLE 156

Fill in the missing letters. Spiral round starting at a corner and spell out a nine-letter word spiralling into the center.

PUZZLE 157

The vowels have been omitted from this trite saying. See if you can complete it.

F T F R S T Y D N T S C
C D W H Y D N T Y G V P

PUZZLE 158

Which diagram A, B, C or D has most in common with the one below?

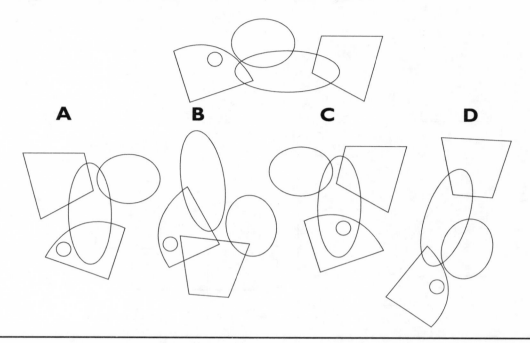

A   **B**   **C**   **D**

PUZZLE 159

Find the numbers to replace the question marks.

31   ?   30   28

A	D	D	D	*29*
B	A	B	D	*27*
C	B	C	B	*?*
A	A	A	A	*32*

PUZZLE 160

Which diagram is the odd one out?

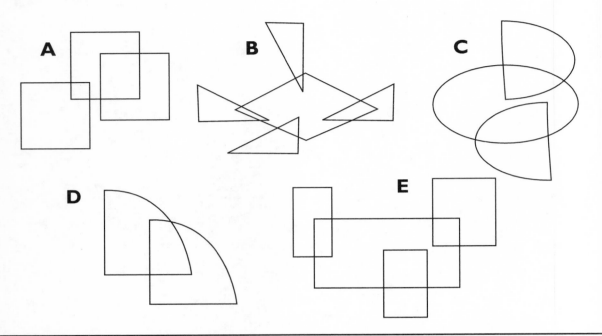

PUZZLE 161

Divide the square into four identical shapes. Each section must contain the same 9 letters which can be arranged into an appropriate 9 letter word.

T	C	M	E	R	I
S	M	I	R	C	T
I	T	Y	Y	E	S
M	R	Y	Y	M	M
S	E	R	I	M	M
C	M	T	C	S	E

PUZZLE 162

Which hexagon is the odd one out

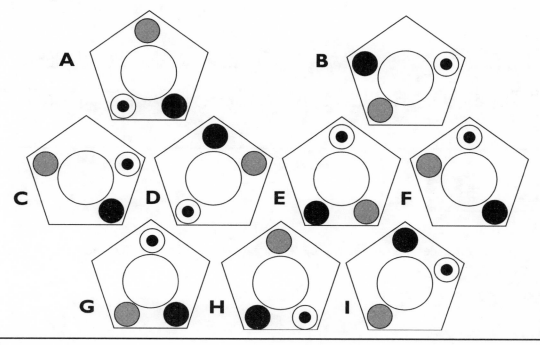

PUZZLE 163

Fill in the missing letters to find this sweet nine-letter word. Start at a corner and spiral in to the center.

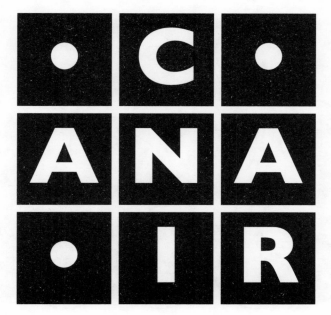

PUZZLE 164

Arrange into 4 groups of three.

FURIES   CAIQUE   WRIT   ORACLE   CANTOR   WHERRY
PAROLE   LORCHA   ESCROW   ARGOSY   ADAGIO   SACKBUT

PUZZLE 165

Each pair of circles produces the circle above by carrying forward only those elements that are different. Similar elements are cancelled out.
Find the circle to replace the question mark.

A   B   C   D   E

PUZZLE 166

Which number should replace the question mark?

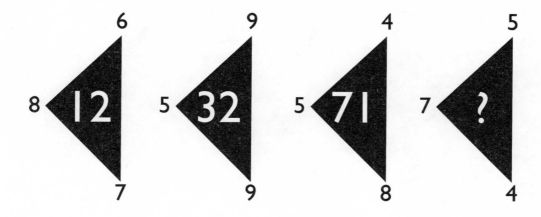

PUZZLE 167

Which number replaces the question mark?

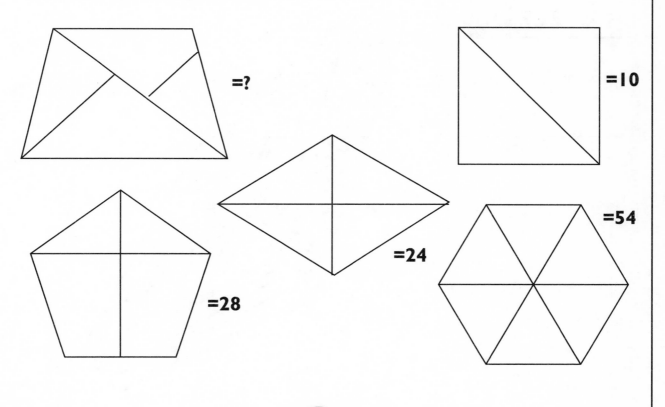

PUZZLE 168

Which is the odd one out?

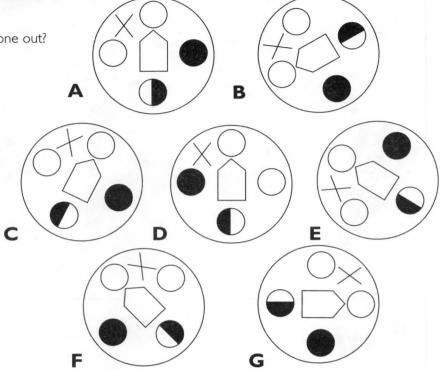

PUZZLE 169

Who is the author of this book?

LEVEL 2

PUZZLE 170

Which is the odd one out?

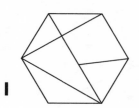
1

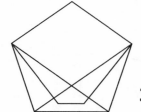
2

3

4

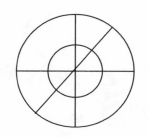
5

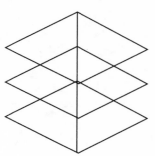
6

7

PUZZLE 171

Place the letters in the grid to make a reptile and a spice.

E
J
M
N
N
O
O
P
R
R
U
T

I

PUZZLE 172

See if you can rearrange this quotation to make sense.

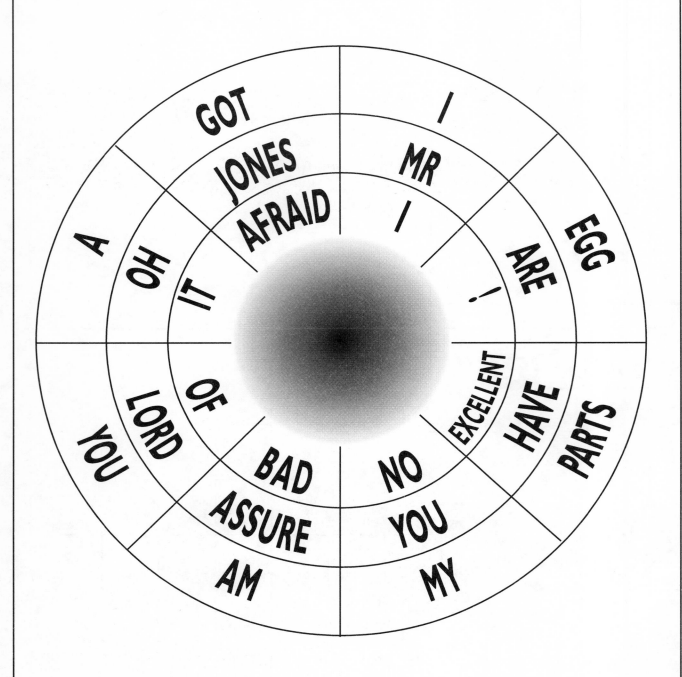

PUZZLE 173

Each line and symbol which appears in the four outer circles is transferred to the center circle according to these rules:

If a line or symbol occurs in the outer circles:

Once:	it is transferred
Twice:	it is possibly transferred
3 Times:	it is transferred
4 Times:	it is not transferred.

Which of the circles A, B, C, D or E should appear at the center of the diagram, above?

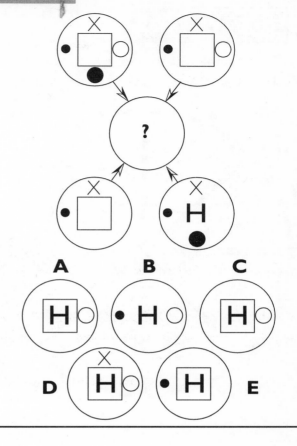

PUZZLE 174

Fill in the missing letters to make a 9-letter word, starting from a corner square and spiral in to the center.

PUZZLE 175

Fill in the blank spaces to find two words which are synonyms.

PUZZLE 176

Fill in the missing letters to find a menu of drinks.

_	H	_	M	_	A	_	N	_
_	I	_	E	U	_	C	_	
_	L	_	V	V	_	T	_	
_	A	_	R	G	_	N	_	
_	P	_	L	J	_	C	_	
_	H	_	C	L	_	T	_	

PUZZLE 177

Which word will fit in front of these words to form new words.

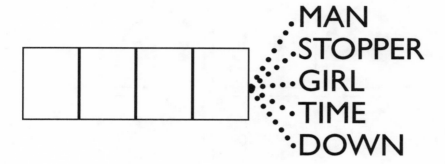

MAN
STOPPER
GIRL
TIME
DOWN

PUZZLE 178

What number should replace the question mark?

A

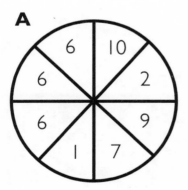

6 · 10
6 · 2
6 · 9
1 · 7

B

7 · 1
2 · 6
8 · 7
4 · 8

C

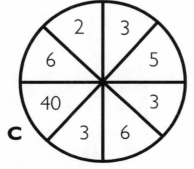

2 · 3
6 · 5
40 · 3
3 · 6

D

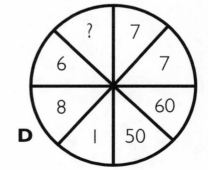

? · 7
6 · 7
8 · 60
1 · 50

PUZZLE 179

Multiply the smallest prime number by the largest odd number.

30	11	77
7	51	19
29	31	37

PUZZLE 180

Find the names of boys and girls by filling in the blanks.

GIRLS

```
_ B _ G _ I _
_ R _ A _ N _
_ N _ A _ E _
_ A _ R _ E _
_ W _ N _ T _
```

BOYS

```
_ E _ B _ R _
_ E _ N _ R _
_ I _ C _ N _
_ I _ F _ E _
_ A _ H _ R _
```

1. D. Only lines which are common to the first two pentagons are carried forward to the final figure, in which they become curved lines.

2

TURN, KEY, WORD, PLAY, BOY
TURNKEY, KEYWORD, WORDPLAY, PLAYBOY

3

```
B A B A N A N B A N B N A N B A
N N N N A B A A A B A N N A A N
A N A B N N B B A N B A N N N A
N A B B A N N N A N A B A B N B
A N A N B A A A A N A B A B A A
B A N A B N A B A A N A A N A N
A B A A B A N A A B A N B A N A
N A A B A N A N B A N B A B A B
A N A N B N B N A B A A N A N A
B A N A A N A A B A A N A N N N
N B B N N N N A N A N A N B A N A
A A N A A B A A N N A A B B A B
B N A B A N A B A B N A N B A N
A B N A B A N B A B N A N B A N
N A A B A N A A A A N B A B N A
A N A N B A B N B A N A N B A N
```

4 C.

5

ANDREW
CLAIRE
HELENA
MARTIN
THOMAS
URSULA

6 B.
The rest are all the same figure rotated.

7 HA
A list of 2-figure square numbers comprising letters assigned to their alphabetic numerical value.

8

9 C.
The contents of each pentagon are determined by the two pentagons below. Where two circles appear in the same position they are not carried forward to the pentagon above.

10

BAKER
TUTOR
EDITOR
PRIEST

11 E.
The rest are the same figure rotated.

12 D. There are four eyes positions: left, right, center and squint. D. completes every possible pairing of the four eye positions.

13 D. Read round each pair of triangles clockwise to spell out four fruits:
CHERRY, ORANGE, RAISIN, DAMSON.

14 To the number 2.
On the top line the totals of the numbers to which the hands point decrease by 2 each time. The numbers on the clock face on the second line are two less than the clocks above them.

15 F.
All the rest have an identical pairing.

16 The letter 'C' is missing from the section containing the letters LOITN. Each circle contains the letters to spell out REAGAN and CLINTON. The letter 'N' in the overlapping portion is shared by both names.

17 A.
Looking down on a standard 6-sided die it is being turned through 45 degrees clockwise each time.

18 JR
Each pair of letters are an equal number of places from the beginning and end of the alphabet respectively.

19 A.
Looking across and down the number of black circles are added to arrive at the number of black circles in the third square. However, with the white circles the number in the second square is deducted from the number in the first square.

20 23
Each number represents the number of empty boxes before it and the number after it, looking along the row.

21 R
The remaining letters are the initials of the planets in our solar system.

22

DALLAS
MOBILE
TOPEKA

	M			D		T	
	O		A			O	
B	L					P	
	E				I	L	
	A	L					K
	A				E	S	

23

CYCLONE
TORNADO
TYPHOON
DROUGHT
RAINBOW

Mixed up word: THUNDER

24 B.
Looking across the time advances 45 minutes each time. Looking down the time goes back 45 minutes each time.

25 BODY MAGNET

26 C.

27

AS YOU LIKE IT
SHAKESPEARE

Reading downwards each number represents two letters of the alphabet according to their position in the alphabet.

1	A	S	19	=	119
19	S	H	8	=	198
25	Y	A	1	=	251

15	O	K	11	=	1511
21	U	E	5	=	215
12	L	S	19	=	1219
9	I	P	16	=	916
11	K	E	5	=	115
5	E	A	1	=	51
9	I	R	18	=	918
20	T	E	5	=	205

28 SEPTEMBER
Jump one month from January to March, then two months from March to June, then three months etc.

29 R.
Take the first letter of the top row with the last letter of the bottom row. Then the second letter of the top row with the penultimate letter of the bottom row etc. When added to the beginning and end of 'ATE', the words: EATEN, WATER, LATEX, HATED, DATED, GATES AND CATER are formed.

30 3A.
All the others have a rotated image pairing.

31 149, 131, 153, 135
in each pair of rows:

A	B	C	D
E	F	G	H

A	+	C	=	F
B	+	D	=	G
A	+	B	=	H
C	+	D	=	E

32 D.
The contents of each pyramid are determined by the contents of the two triangles below it. Only when two black, or two white dots appear in the same position are they carried forward to the pyramid above, where they change from black to white, or vice versa.

33 He loved MARYLAND.
He loved the ones with girls' names embedded in them, i.e. INDIANA, but hated the ones with boys' names, i.e. KENTUCKY.

34 The hand should point to 11. The totals of the numbers which the arrows poiont to on each clock face increase by 3 each time: 14, 17, 20, 23.

35 D.
A has the same figures as C turned upside down, and in reverse order. B has the same figures as E turned upside down, and in reverse order.

36 WEDNESDAY

37 E.
The top left-hand corner dot moves round one corner at a time clockwise. The top right-hand corner dot moves backwards and forwards to two corners. The bottom left-hand corner dot moves round one corner at a time anti-clockwise. The bottom right-hand corner dot moves backwards and forwards to two corners.

38 ANNIVERSARY

39 C.
In all the others, the top half is a mirror image of the bottom half.

40
PIE
DIE
DUE
HUE
HUMBLE

41 2119
The number following each word working clockwise is determined by the position of the letters of the word in the alphabet.

U=21   S=19   =2119

42 B.
It is only one which cannot be folded to form a cube.

43 167
2x8=16 } 167
63 / 9=7
similarly

4x3=12} 128
56 / 7 =8
6x 9 =54 } 548
48 / 6 =8

44

HI HOH I I OHOHH I OH I
I HOHO I O I I OHH I HH I
OO I HHO I I O I I OH I HO
HOOOO I OH I H I I I HO I
I O I OH I HO I I O I I OH I
HOO I O I OHO I I O I H I O
O I HHH I I OHHO I OH I
I OH I I O I I I OH I I H I O
I O I O I I O I I OO I OO I H
HO I I OHO I I OO I I O I H
I OO I O I O I I I I HOH I H
O I OO I O I O I O I O I O
HOO I OOHOH I OO I I O I
I H I O I I I H I OO I H I I O
H I O I I I OOH I H I OOHO
OHO I OO I H I O I HH I H I

45 D.

46 B.
G is the same as E
A is the same as F
C is the same as D

47
MIDGE
EMMET
APHID
LOUSE
DRONE

48 4. Corner dice are subtracted from each other to obtain middle faces.

49 Start square

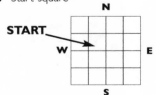

50
ALDER
BIRCH
HAZEL
MAPLE
ROWAN

51 2A
There should be a • at the top of the circle.

52

The bottle moves 45°, then 90°, then 135°, then 180°, and finally, the solution distance of 225°

53 27

54 7
In each vertical column the 3 smaller numbers add up to the large number.

55 D.
In any row or column the last figure contains only the elements common to both preceeding figures.

56
Two series beginning at 32, the first increases by one each step, the other decreases by one.

57 6
The corresponding sections of the three wheels add up to 19.

58 $22
Vowels	=	$1
Consonants	=	$4

59 C.

60 34.
7x7 = 49. 3x5 = 15.
49-15 = 34

61   GUPPY
           LUPIN

62 GRAPPA

63 C.
Each bottom pair of circles are added to produce the circle above.
But not like symbols.

64 ENUMERATE

65   AROMATIC
           PERFUMED

66   HOTELIER

67 C.
Starting at the bottom circle combine figures, but dropping any repeated elements.

68 17
(11+12+9+1)-(5+3+6+2)

69   CASSEROLE
           FRICASSEE
           MINCEMEAT
           SCHNITZEL
           SPAGHETTI
           HAMBURGER

70 32

71 D.

72 SWEET

73 7
In corresponding parts of each segment
A-B+C=D
8-2+1=7

74 2
The number relates to the number of shapes in which the number is enclosed.

75   AUBRETIA
           GLADIOLA
           DIANTHUS
           BLUEBELL

76 No. He disliked places with an i in the name.

77 1162
83x14=1162

78 55
5x5=1
4x4=4
3x3=9
2x2=16
1x1=25
55

79 Start at 26 then add 6 then deduct 4 until by spiralling in towards the center end at 46.

80   EPHRAIM
          AARON
          SHADRACH
          ABRAHAM
          HEROD
          BATHSHEBA
          BENJAMIN
          SAUL
          JOSEPH
          MOSES

81 Midway between 4D and 4E divide the lakes.
5 to the east, 5 to the west
5 to the north, 5 to the south

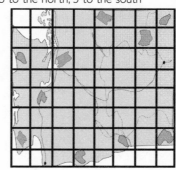

82
1.	IMPALA
2.	ONAGER
3.	RHESUS
4.	PANTHER
5.	ELAND

83 ATE

84 12.5
There are 2 series
$(+3^1/_2)$ 2 $5^1/_2$ 9 $12^1/_2$
$(-1^1/_4)$ 11 $9^3/_4$ $8^1/_2$ $7^1/_4$

85 Take pi as $^{22}/_7$
Then C = $^{22}/_7 \times 28 = 88$ ins.
Number of revolutions
= $1760 \times 3 \times {}^{12}/_{88} = 720$

86 SCUBA
It contains a creature, as do:
CLASPING
PAPERS
SEWED
SKIDDED
TOXIC

87 B.

88 Take reciprocal
1	2 hours	1/2	=.5
2	3 hours	1/3	=.333
3	4 hours	1/4	=.25
4	6 hours	1/6	=.166
1.25
Again take reciprocal
1/1.25   =.8
Answer   .8 hours

89
Trees	Body	Colours	Fish
Cypress	Tarsus	Saffron	Anchovy
Aniseed	Scapula	Sorrel	Herring
Hemlock	Fibula	Claret	Lamprey

90 C.

91 9
The total in each column increases by
1 each time: 6, 7, 8, 9

92 D.

93 D.
It contains the letters EFH
The others contain consecutive letters
of the alaphabet:
LMN, VWX, XYZ, KLM

94   PICCOLO
CLARINET
BASSOON

95 It was instant coffee and he hadn't
yet added the water.

96 B.
The upward pointing triangle is moving
continually from left to right, the
downward pointing triangle and the
black dot continually change places.

97 4
The first two numbers in each line or
column are divided by either 4 or 3,
whichever is possible and the
quotients added together to produce
the third number.
E.g.   (8 / 4) + (12 / 3) = 6

98 208
Take the numbers corresponding with
the position in the alphabet of the first
two letters of each day of the week
starting Sunday (S19, U21).
THURSDAY = T20, H8 (208).

99 E.
There are four circles, two are black
and two are white. The largest circle
and the smallest circle are white and
the two middle size circles are black.

100 He is a mailman who delivers
letters to the different foreign
embassies in the United States. The
land of an embassy belongs to the
country of the embassy.

101 ORBIT
Select letters from either side in the
same sequence that generated
ADORN, ie, just as A is the 4th letter
in DYNAMIC, so is O the 4th in
RETORTS, etc.

102 562
In all the others multiply the first and
last digits and divide by 2 to arrive at
the middle digit.

103 B.
Only when a dot appears in the same
position in just two of the squares is it
carried forward to the final square, but
changes from white to black and vice
versa.

104   CALICO
MUSLIN
SATEEN
ALPACA
VELVET
MOHAIR (Scrambled)

105 4
$7 \times 6 = 42 + 4 = 46$
Similarly
$8 \times 7 = 56 + 2 = 58$

106 E.
It contains only two small white circles.
The rest contain three.

107 C.

108 33
Divide the first number by 2 and the
second by 3 and add together.
54   2 = 27
18   3 = 6   27 + 6 = 33

109 He had hiccups and that is why
he asked for the water. The shock of
seeing the gun cured him quicker.

110 O
The letters in the circle convert the
other words to birds:
HACK	HAWK
ROCK	ROOK
DOME	DOVE
COLT	COOT

111 B.
At each stage an extra line is added
spiralling inwards. The spiral alternates
clockwise then anti-clockwise in turn.

112 3 + 1 × 4 - 1 / 5 + 9 / 2 = 6

113 BEAN SPROUT

LEVEL 2 ANSWERS

114 10
Take the difference between the number of sides in each pair of figures and multiply by 2.

115 175
The four largest numbers in the disc are arrived at by doubling the four smaller numbers + 1.

116 The letter 'O'. He is juggling with colored balls, one for each color of the rainbow:
Red, orange, yellow, green, blue, indigo, violet.

117 11
O has 14 letters in front of it in the alphabet and 11 behind.
J has 9 in front and 16 behind.

118 A.

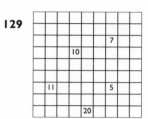

119 2
If the alphabet were written in a circle the numbers would represent half the number of spaces from one letter to the next.

120 B.
So that one triangle, a large circle and a small circle all contain a dot.

121
```
P I T E O T E I T I P T O T E
P O I I I E O T O P O T I I I
I T E P P I T O P E E P P P P
T I P T I E I P T O T E I T P
P P O I T T O I I I I T E E I
O I T P E T E T E P E I P O T
E I T E T P T P I O O E E T O
P O P O O E T O T T O O P O T
E E T T E T I E P T P T O P I
T I T P O P P I T O O T T T P
O P O T O T T I T P P O E I T
E P O T I T P O T I I I O P O
P T P P P P E T I P O T E P
I I T I T O T T I T P O E O I
T P T T O P T O E T I P E T T
```

122

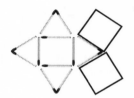

123 10. Allocate the numbers at the corners of the triangle to letters of the alphabet.
19-9-24 spells six
20-23-15 spells two
20-5-14 spells ten

124 BREWERY.
All the words in the left-hand box contain names of animals:
DEMURE (EMU)
AMULET (MULE)
MORATORIUM (RAT)
MULTIGRAM (TIGER)
BREWERY (EWE).

125 B.
The small dot moves one forward two back.
The upward triangle moves one back two forward.
The downward triangle moves one forward two back.

126 MORBID HEAP

127 Brian and Cathy were hurricanes.

128 All constructions:
LODGE
TOWER
CASTLE
TEMPLE

129

						7	
			10				
	11					5	
				20			

130 ENGINE
Select letters from either side in the same sequence that generated DAMSEL, ie, just as D is the 4th letter in BUNDLE, so is E the 4th in SCREEN, etc.

131 B.

132 89
Start at 1 and working clockwise double the previous number and add 1, then 2, then 3, etc.

133 MADISON

134 He had left an envelope with his name and address written on, in the pocket of his old jeans.

135 2
Every square block of numbers totals 15

136 3B

137 MADRID

138 B.
The sequence is -2, +1 dots and +3, -1 lines

139 MAGNET
SWITCH
SOCKET
STATIC
AERIAL
DYNAMO

140 A.
Add elements across rows and down columns.

141 J
A → E → I → M → Q (+ 4 spaces)
Z → V → R → N → J (– 4 spaces)

142 MY ANSWER

143 E.
Add elements across rows and down columns, but similar symbols disappear.

144 23 UNITS
Each car purchased a number of units which was the square root of its number plate.

145 17 - 4 = 13
To find the number in adjoining circles
If both are even add them
If both are odd multiply them
If one is odd and one is even subtract them.

146 E.
Add elements across rows and down column, but similar symbols disappear.

147 Circle 1 15 odd one out
$9^3 = 729$
$11^3 = 1331$
$13^3 = 2197$
Circle 2 18 odd one out
$8^2 = 64$
$12^2 = 144$
$16^2 = 256$

148 75
Each number is obtained by adding the two previous numbers + 1.

149 It is the only shape consisting of an odd number of sides.

150 ⊢ In each column the top symbol in the previous column disappears and the remainder are turned upside down.

151 C.

152 CAUTIONED
Because all words in A contain all five vowels.

153
127	+	453	580
371	+	596	967
245	+	619	864

154
5, 6, 7, 8
in any position.
The completed square contains the following
1	×	1
2	×	2
3	×	3
4	×	4
5	×	5
6	×	6
7	×	7
8	×	8

155 B.

156 TELEPHONE

157 "If at first you do not succeed why don't you give up?"

158 D.
It is a rotated mirror image of the top diagram.

159
29	top	
30	side	
A	=	8
B	=	6
C	=	9
D	=	7

160 A.
The small pieces in the other diagrams equal the large piece except A.

161 SYMMETRIC

T	C	M	E	R	I
S	M	I	R	C	T
I	T	Y	Y	E	S
M	R	Y	Y	M	M
S	E	R	I	M	M
C	M	T	C	S	E

162 F.
A is the same as I
B is the same as E
C is the same as H
D is the same as G

163 SACCHARIN

164
Mythology:
FURIES   ORACLE   ARGOSY
Law:
ESCROW   WRIT   PAROLE
Music
SACKBUT   ADAGIO   CANTOR
Boats
LORCHA   WHERRY   CAIQUE

165 E.

166 61
The three outside numbers are added and then reversed.

167 28
Number of lines × Number of areas
7 × 4 = 28

168 D.
A is the same as G
B is the same as F
C is the same as E

169 SHAKESPEARE
Each letter shown on the spine has been advanced two letters
i.e. S + 2 = U
Each letter shown on the cover for the title has been advanced one letter
i.e. U + 1 = T

170 2. Only 1 figure has an odd number of spaces:

1	-	6 spaces
2	-	7 spaces
3	-	10 spaces
4	-	8 spaces
5	-	8 spaces
6	-	8 spaces
7	-	12 spaces

171 JUNIPER
MONITOR

172 I am afraid you have got a bad egg Mr Jones. Oh no my Lord I assure you! Parts of it are excellent.

173 C.

174 ANONYMOUS

175
ADMONISH
REPROACH

176
CHAMPAGNE
LIMEJUICE
SLIVOVITZ
TARRAGONA
APPLEJACK
CHOCOLATE

177
SHOW

178 40
Incorresponding segments of the circle
A x B - C = D

179 539.
7 x 77 = 539

180

GIRLS	BOYS
ABIGAIL	HERBERT
ARIADNE	LEONARD
ANNABEL	VINCENT
HARRIET	WILFRED
GWYNETH	ZACHARY

LEVEL 3

PUZZLE 1

What letter replaces the question mark?

PUZZLE 2

 **is to**  **as** 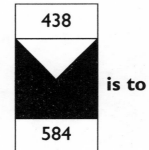 **is to**

A	B	C	D

PUZZLE 3

What letter should replace the question mark?

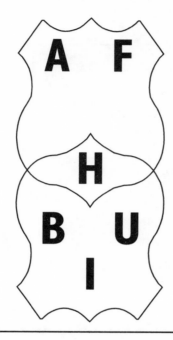

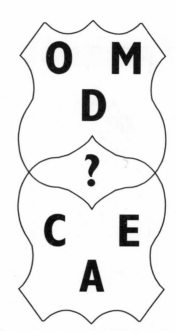

PUZZLE 4

What is the missing number?

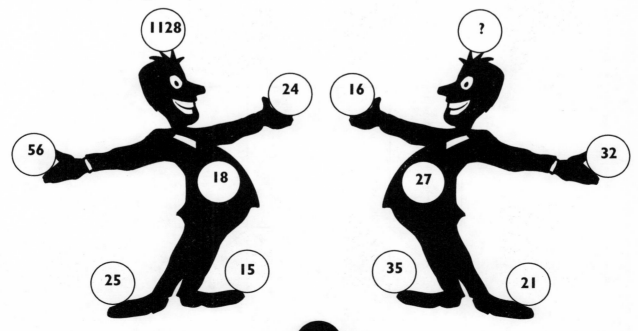

PUZZLE 5

What should appear in the box with the question mark?

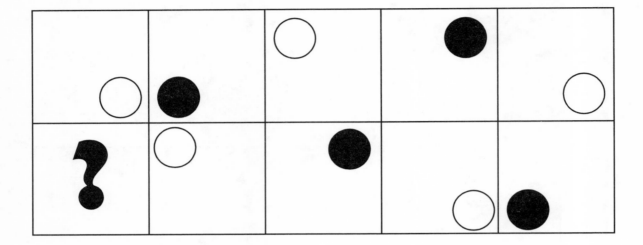

PUZZLE 6

What should appear instead of the question mark?

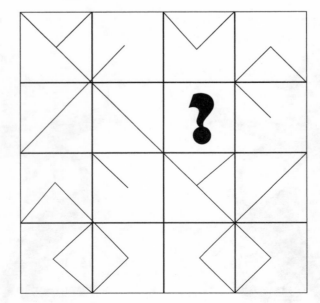

PUZZLE 7

What letter should replace the question mark?

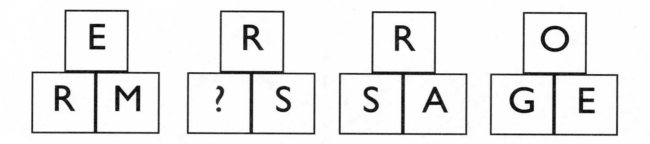

PUZZLE 8

A mysterious crate has arrived full of a certain product. Someone has scribbled anagrams of the product and its inventor on the side of the crate. Can you unscramble the anagrams to find what is in the box?

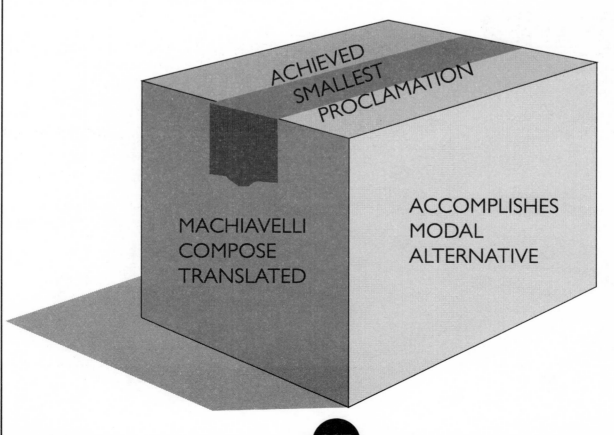

PUZZLE 9

What number should replace the question mark?

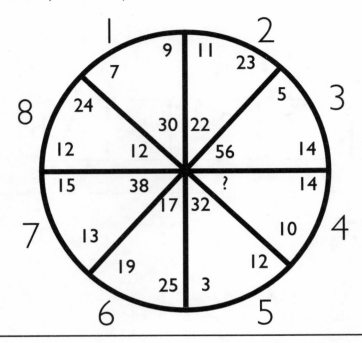

PUZZLE 10

What letter should appear in the middle of the star?

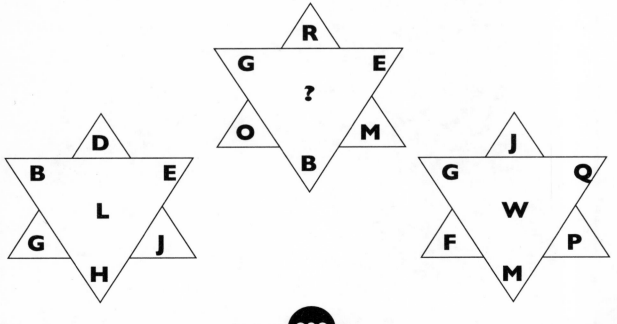

PUZZLE 11

Which is the odd one out?

A   B   C

D   E   F

PUZZLE 12

What number should replace the question mark?

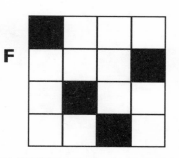
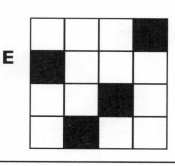

12   16

16

21   20   18   8

35   ?

PUZZLE 13

Can you work out the pattern of this grid and fill in the missing section?

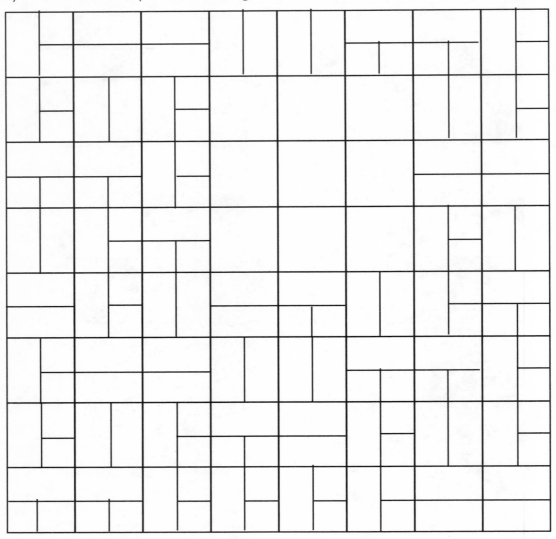

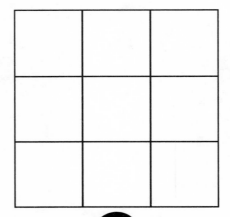

PUZZLE 14

Which pair of letters is missing from the bottom right hand corner of the fourth square?

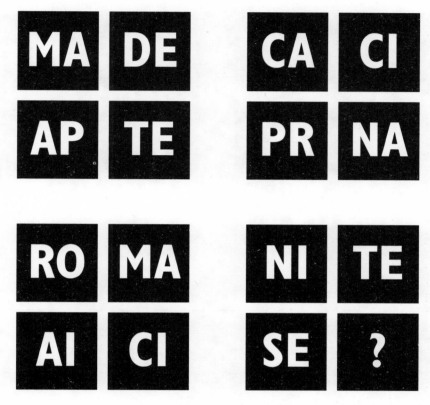

PUZZLE 15

What should be the contents of the final box?

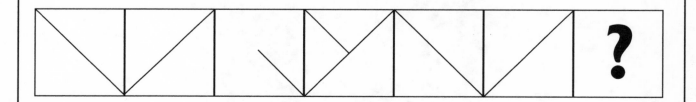

PUZZLE 16

Which anagrammed book title is the odd one out?

SCAN OUR OIL

BUY GRAND BEAR

VIOLET WRIST

RIDDEN WOOD

PUZZLE 17

What number is missing from the circle?

51
61
55
?
5
4
105
9
106

PUZZLE 18

The numbers 1,2,5,8,2,1,4,8,3 are arranged in a sequence, however some numbers are out of order. Shade in these numbers to reveal another number. What is it?

8	5	1	3	4	1	8	5	1	3	4	1	8	5	1
2	2	2	8	8	2	2	2	2	8	8	2	2	2	2
1	1	5	4	3	8	1	1	5	4	3	8	1	1	5
4	3	8	2	5	5	4	3	8	1	1	5	4	3	8
8	8	2	8	2	2	8	8	2	2	2	2	8	8	2
3	4	1	2	1	1	3	4	1	8	5	1	3	4	1
1	1	4	5	2	3	1	1	4	5	8	3	1	1	4
2	2	8	1	8	8	2	2	8	2	2	8	2	2	8
5	8	3	1	1	4	5	8	3	1	1	4	5	8	3
8	5	1	3	4	1	8	5	1	3	4	1	8	5	1
2	2	2	8	8	2	2	2	2	8	8	2	2	2	2
1	1	5	4	3	8	1	1	5	4	3	8	1	1	5
4	3	8	1	1	5	4	3	8	1	1	5	4	3	8
8	8	2	2	2	2	8	8	2	2	2	2	8	8	2
3	4	1	8	5	1	3	4	1	8	5	1	3	4	1

LEVEL 3

PUZZLE 19

Which figure should replace the question mark?

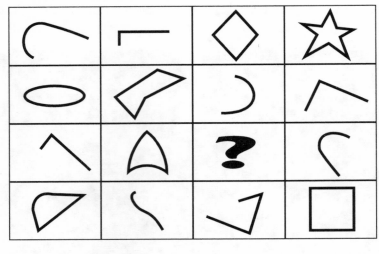

PUZZLE 20

Take a letter from each shield in turn to find five words connected with heraldry. Then rearrange the remaining letters to find a sixth heraldic term.

LEVEL 3

PUZZLE 21

What number is missing from the circle?

835   11
13
?

15   964
13
10

PUZZLE 22

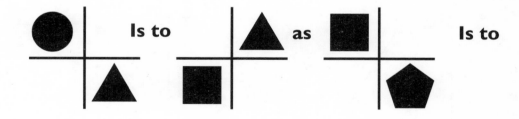

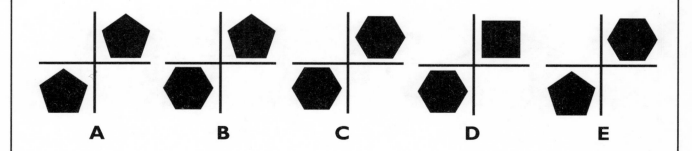

A   B   C   D   E

215

PUZZLE 23

What number is missing from the right circle?

Left circle: 4785 23 25 3219 7643 22 24 2863

Right circle: 5963 7468 24 15 ? 8493 20 9436

PUZZLE 24

Six of these pieces will construct the letter 'H'. Which is the redundant piece?

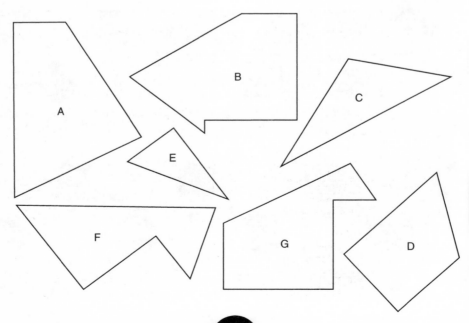

PUZZLE 25

Which piece is missing to construct a circle?

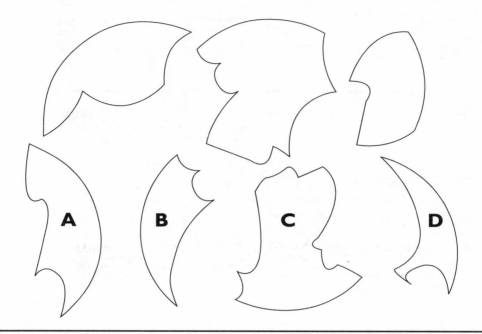

PUZZLE 26

What should be contained in place of the question mark?

LEVEL 3

PUZZLE 27

Discover the logic behind the pattern of numbers and letters in this grid.

		13			
				25	D
		G			
					46
		53		?	
	H				

What letter should replace the question mark and where would you place number 21 in the grid?

PUZZLE 28

Which number does not belong in the circle?

197 451 756 629
754 129 298 567 385
236 296 791 145 928
475 632 583

PUZZLE 29

Insert the missing letter in each grid.

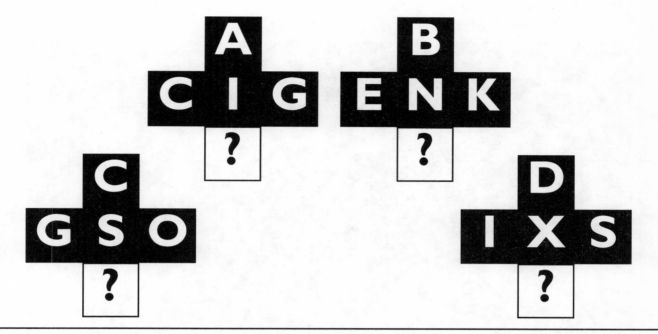

PUZZLE 30

Which is the odd one out?

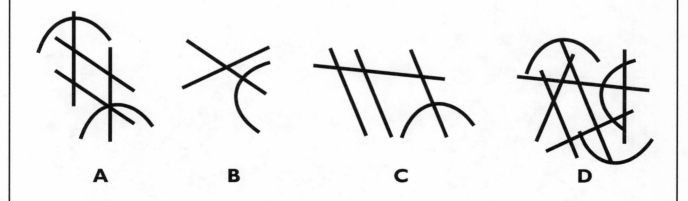

A   B   C   D

LEVEL 3

PUZZLE 31

The grid follows the pattern: 2, 6, 3, 0, 8, 4, 3, 1, 7, however some of the numbers have been increased by one. If you highlight these numbers, what letter will appear?

```
6 3 0 8 4 3 1 7 2 6 3 0 8 4 3
2 7 2 6 3 0 8 4 3 1 7 2 6 3 1
7 1 1 7 2 6 3 0 8 4 3 1 7 0 7
1 3 3 1 7 2 6 3 0 8 4 3 2 8 2
3 4 4 3 7 2 6 3 0 8 4 1 6 4 6
4 8 8 4 1 6 3 0 8 4 3 7 3 3 3
8 0 0 8 3 3 8 4 3 4 1 2 0 1 0
0 3 3 0 4 8 0 8 1 2 7 6 8 7 8
3 6 6 3 8 2 4 7 3 8 2 3 4 2 4
6 2 2 6 0 3 4 8 0 3 6 0 3 6 3
2 7 7 2 3 6 2 7 1 3 4 8 1 3 1
7 1 1 7 1 3 4 8 0 3 6 2 7 0 7
1 3 3 4 8 0 3 6 2 7 1 3 4 8 2
3 4 8 0 3 6 2 7 1 3 4 8 0 3 6
4 8 0 3 6 2 7 1 3 4 8 0 3 6 2
```

PUZZLE 32

What should appear in the missing square?

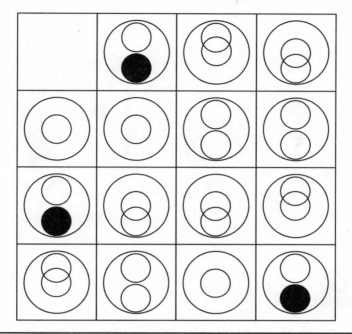

PUZZLE 33

Which letter does not belong in this triangle?

S
S · L
S · A · C
I · E · E · O

PUZZLE 34

Which number does not belong in the fourth pentagon?

PUZZLE 35

CALM= 8

BACK = 4

PALE = 9

RACE = ?

What number should replace the question mark?

PUZZLE 36

Which four of the pieces below can be fitted together to for a perfect square?

PUZZLE 37

Which pentagon is missing from the top of the pyramid?

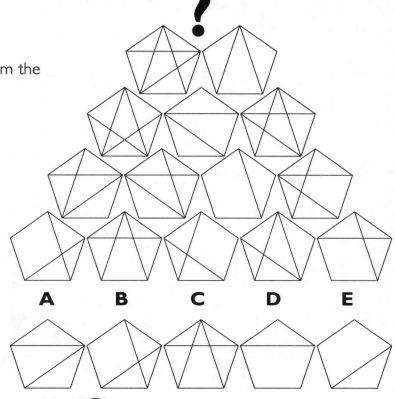

A   B   C   D   E

PUZZLE 38

The caseload of books arrived with some very strange messages written on the sides. Actually each message is an anagram of the book contained within the case and it's author. Can you work out what book is inside the case?

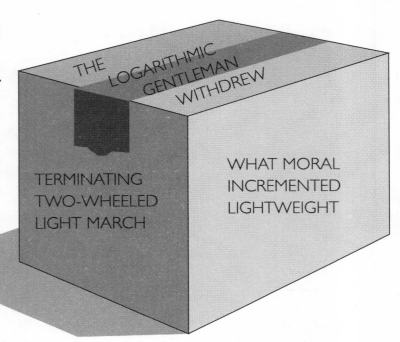

THE LOGARITHMIC GENTLEMAN WITHDREW

TERMINATING TWO-WHEELED LIGHT MARCH

WHAT MORAL INCREMENTED LIGHTWEIGHT

PUZZLE 39

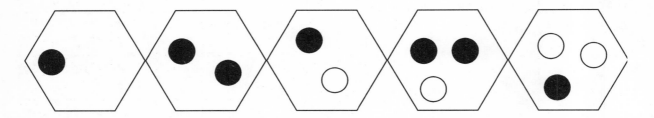

Which hexagon comes next?

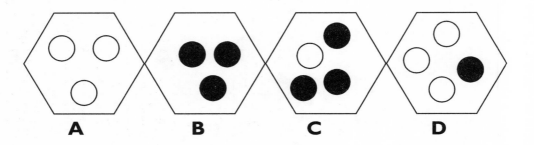

A   B   C   D

PUZZLE 40

What number should replace the question mark?

12	14	15	36
26	?	14	21
19	36	90	17
15	21	12	84

PUZZLE 41

You must find the starting point and visit every square once each only and finish at the square containing the treasure marked T. 2W3S means you must move 2 west 3 south.

1E 1S	1W 2S	1E 2S	2S 3E	2S 2W	2E 1S	3S 3W	1S 2W
2E 5S	2S 3E	**T**	2W 2S	3S 2W	1N 2W	1N 1W	1S 6W
2E 3S	1N 1E	2N 1W	3W 4S	2N 2E	1W 2S	1W 2S	1N 3W
3N 2E	1W 2S	3N 2W	2S 2W	3N 3E	1N 1W	3N 2W	1W 2S
1N 2E	3N 5E	1N 2W	2S 2W	1E 2S	2W 2S	1E 2N	2N 2W
1N 1E	1E 2S	4N 2W	2N 2E	2N 3E	1E 2S	2W 2S	2S 7W
1S 3E	5N 2E	1N 2E	1S 2E	1S 3E	1S 4W	2N 1E	3N 1W
3N 3E	3N 1W	1N 2E	1N 3E	1E 2N	1N 2E	1E 2N	3N 1W

PUZZLE 42

Working clockwise take one letter from each circle in turn to spell out three famous explorers. One word of warning, each of the names starts in a different circle.

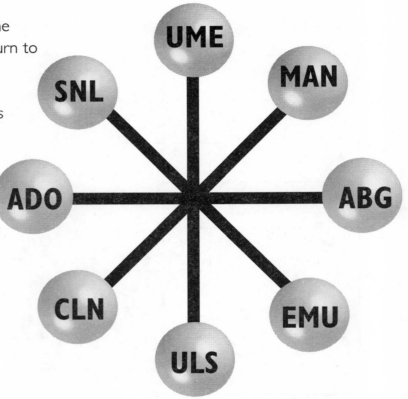

UME
MAN
SNL
ABG
ADO
CLN
EMU
ULS

PUZZLE 43

Which of the words is the odd one out?

DISMISS
WAYLAY
FURTHER
REMAIN
BACKPACK

PUZZLE 44

Work out the reasoning behind this grid and fill in the missing section.

```
Z  T  T  P  Y  X  L  K  K  Y  Z  T  T  P  Y  X
Y  T  P  Y  X  L  K  K  Y  Z  T  T  P  Y  X  L
K  T  T  P  Y  X  L  K  K  Y  Z  T  T  P  Y  K
K  Z  T  Z  T  T  P  Y  X  L  K  K  Y  Z  X  K
L  Y  Z  Y  L  K  K  Y  Z  T  T  P  Y  T  L  Y
X  K  Y  K  X  Z  T  T  P  Y  X  L  X  T  K  Z
Y  K  K  K  Y  Y  T  P  Y  X  ?  ?  ?  P  K  T
P  L  K  L  P  K  T  T  P  Y  ?  ?  ?  Y  Y  T
T  X  L  X  T  K  Z  T  Z  X  ?  ?  ?  X  Z  P
T  Y  X  Y  T  L  Y  K  K  L  Y  Z  Y  L  T  Y
Z  P  Y  P  Z  X  Y  P  T  T  Z  T  Z  K  T  X
Y  T  P  T  Y  K  K  L  X  Y  P  T  T  K  P  L
K  T  T  T  Z  Y  K  K  L  X  Y  P  T  Y  Y  K
K  Z  T  Z  Y  K  K  L  X  Y  P  T  T  Z  X  K
L  Y  K  K  L  X  Y  P  T  T  Z  Y  K  K  L  Y
X  Y  P  T  T  Z  Y  K  K  L  X  Y  P  T  T  Z
```

PUZZLE 45

Which is the odd one out?

A   **B**   **C**   **D**   **E**

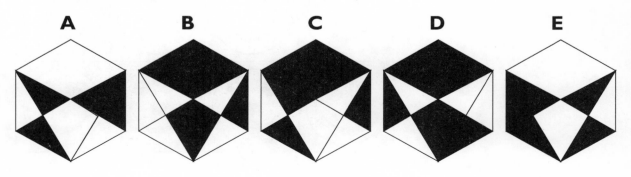

PUZZLE 46

Each line and symbol which appears in the four outer circles is transferred to the center circle according to these rules:

If a line or symbol occurs in the outer circles:

once:	it is transferred
twice:	it is possibly transferred
3 times:	it is transferred
4 times:	it is not transferred

Which of the circles A, B, C, D or E, should appear at the center of the diagram?

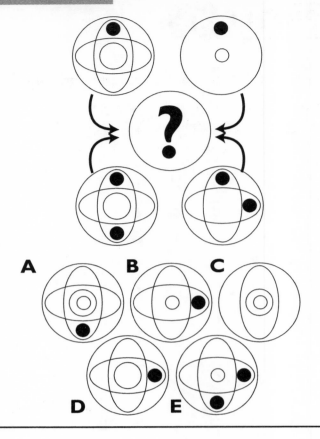

A   B   C

D   E

PUZZLE 47

Find the face to take the place of the question mark. The route starts at a corner square and spirals into the center.

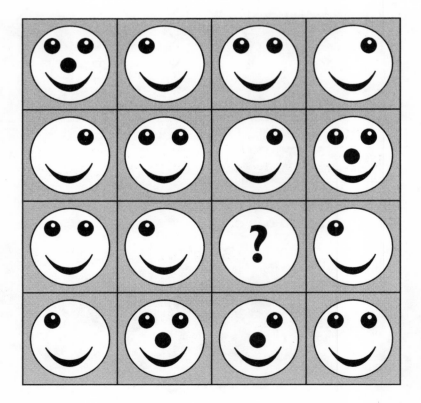

LEVEL 3

PUZZLE 48

Each pair of circles produces the circle above by carrying forward only those elements that are different. Similar elements are cancelled out.
Find the circle to replace the question mark.

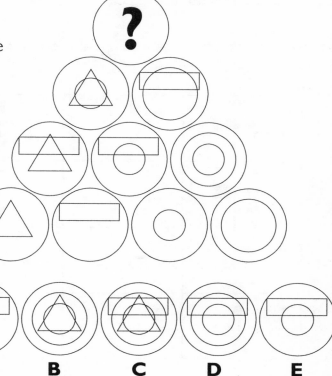

A   B   C   D   E

PUZZLE 49

Where was car E going to?

A.
Oakland to Denver

B.
Sacramento to Ottawa

C.
Boston to Nebraska

D.
Dallas to Seattle

E.
Minneapolis to:
Kentucky
Springfield
Baton Rouge
Tallahassee
Washington

LEVEL 3

PUZZLE 50

Work out the pattern of the route and find out what should replace the question mark.

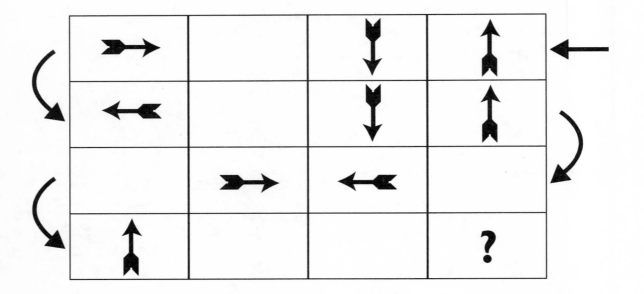

PUZZLE 51

In segment 8 where should you place ⊙ to keep in sequence?

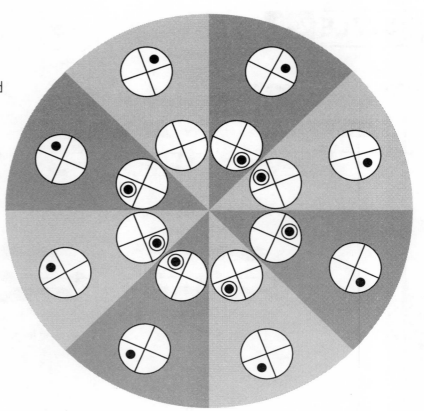

230

PUZZLE 52

This is an anagram of a bird. We have given you the letters that you do not need. Find the missing letters, change their order, and you will find a bird.

Z U D B V K
S Q I X H
T J W P M Y

PUZZLE 53

What number should replace the question mark.

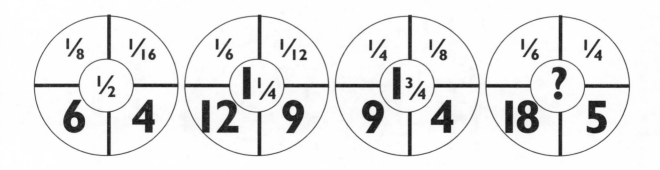

PUZZLE 54

Which circle should replace the question mark?

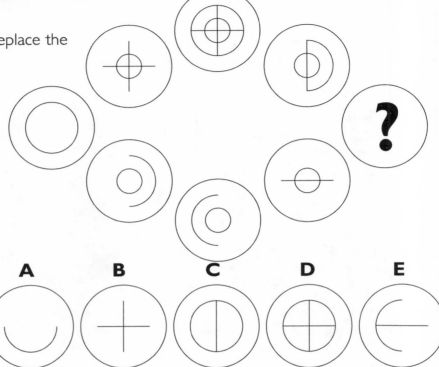

A   B   C   D   E

PUZZLE 55

Which of these is not an anagram of currency?

TENAVOC

DILGRUE

STRIPEA

IRADIEN

MILREID

PUZZLE 56

Which circle's letters cannot be rearranged into a 6-letter word?

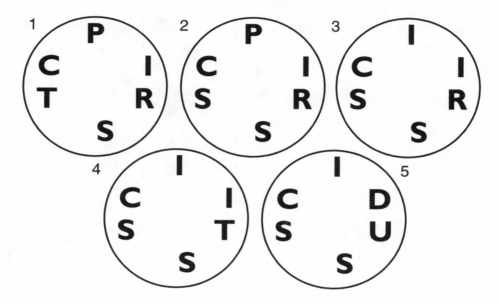

PUZZLE 57

Spell out a 10-letter word by moving into each circle once only.
Clue: A ship.

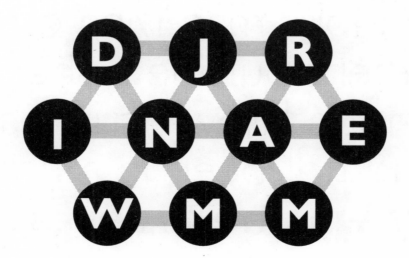

PUZZLE 58

Which cube cannot be made from this pattern?

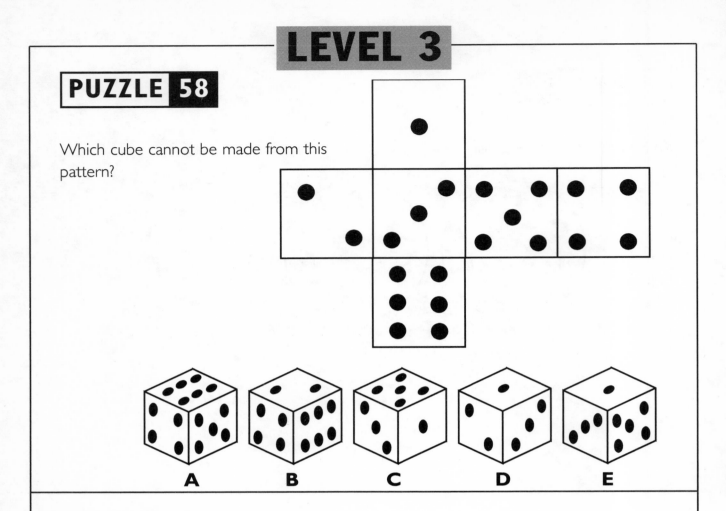

A   **B**   **C**   **D**   **E**

PUZZLE 59

A policeman arrested an unconsious man lying on the pavement outside a shop. He was not a known criminal and he had not been in a fight. **Why was he arrested?**

PUZZLE 60

Which hexagon is the odd one out ?

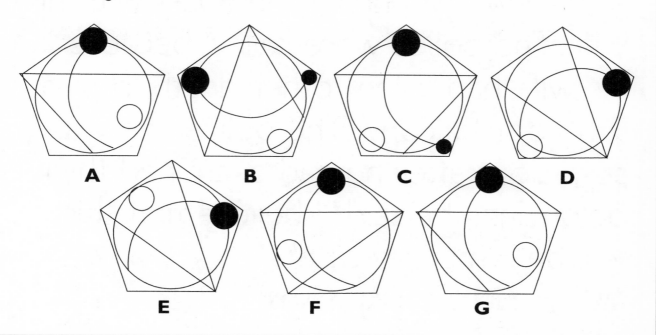

PUZZLE 61

Unravel the logic behind this diagram and find which symbol should go into the squares marked with a question mark.

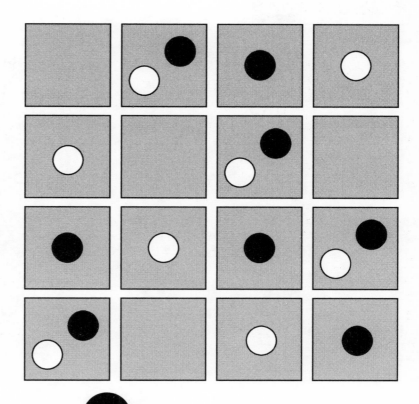

PUZZLE 62

A man was on holiday in Spain with his wife. The police were called, because his wife had fallen to her death from a 9th floor balcony. The policeman was suspicious after he had examined their belongings, he said "I believe that this will be a murder case"
Why did he say that ?

PUZZLE 63

Which fish should start the first box? Take from the second box, to a definite rule.

FIRST

?
REMORA
ANGEL
SQUID
SOLE
EEL

SECOND

PLAICE
CAPLIN
WHITING
GUNNEL
KIPPER

PUZZLE 64

Which is the odd one out?

165   286
374   693
572   891
792   143
      471

PUZZLE 65

Can you work out what number the missing hour hand should point to on clock 5?

1

2

3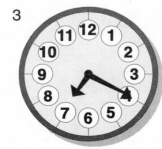

4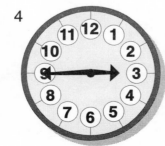

5

PUZZLE 66

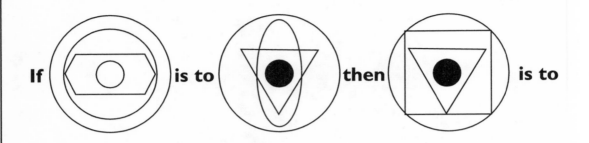

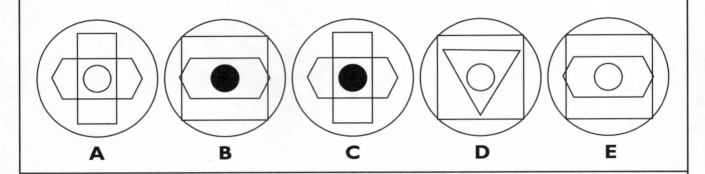

| A | B | C | D | E |

PUZZLE 67

Can you work out which number should replace the question mark?

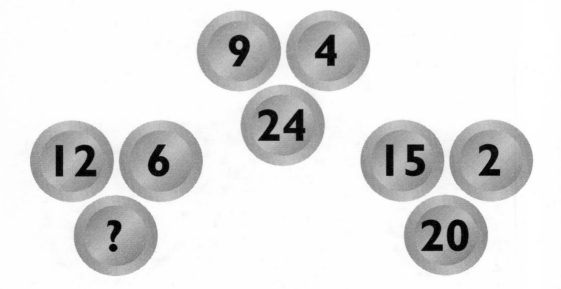

PUZZLE 68

Can you find the number that should replace the question mark?

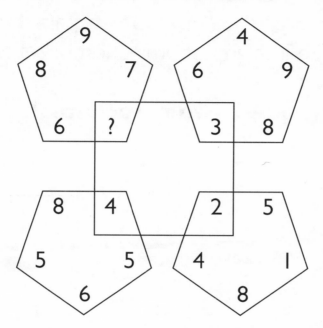

PUZZLE 69

Can you find the odd one out?

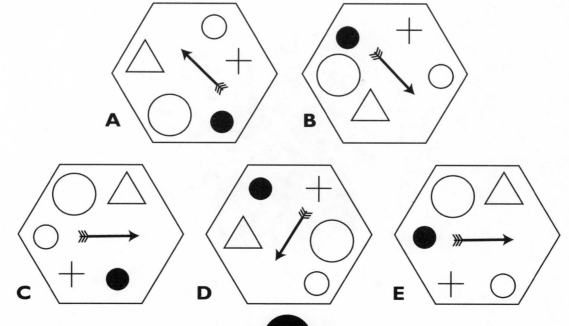

PUZZLE 70

A plane was hijacked and the hijacker instructed the pilot to fly to a certain airport to pick up two parachutes and a $50,000 package in high denomination bills, then fly on.

Why did he request two parachutes?

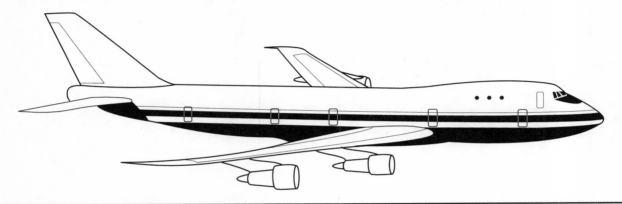

PUZZLE 71

Can you work out which number should replace the question mark?

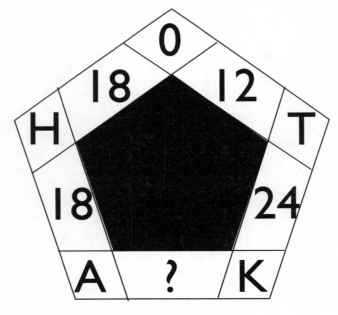

PUZZLE 72

Can you replace the question mark with a number to a definite rule?

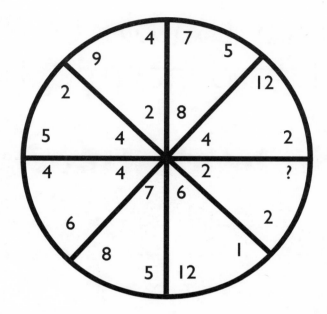

PUZZLE 73

What value weight should be placed at D to balance the scale?

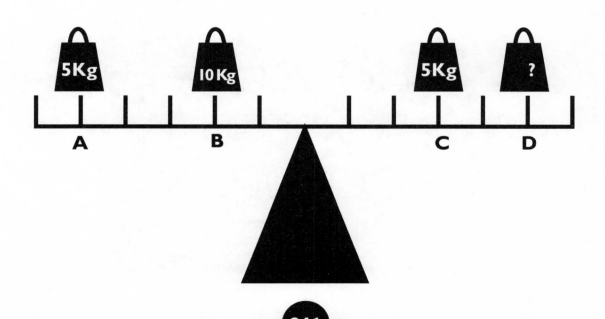

PUZZLE 74

A man writes a check and then tears it into 185 pieces and posts it to a department store.

Why did he do that?

PUZZLE 75

These are anagrams of fish, but one is a bird, can you find it?

RABBLE

TOBBUR

NOGGUD

PORREGU

OCCOUK

WINNOM

PUZZLE 76

Each line and symbol which appears in the four outer circles is transferred to the center circle according to these rules:

If a line or symbol occurs in the outer circles:

Once	it is transferred
Twice	it is possibly transferred
3 times	it is transferred
4 times	it is not transferred.

Which of the circles A, B, C, D or E, should appear at the center of the diagram?

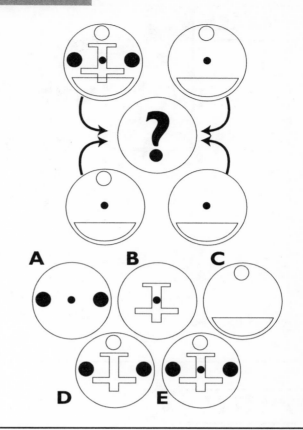

PUZZLE 77

Select one letter from each pentagon in turn and find five 6-letter animals.

PUZZLE 78

If
$$N + N + M = 14$$
$$L + L + K = 20$$
$$M + K + N = 12$$
$$N + K + L = 18$$

What is the value of K?

PUZZLE 79

Which square completes the series?

   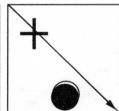 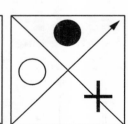

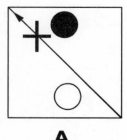 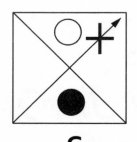  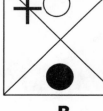

A   **B**   **C**   **D**

PUZZLE 80

Which circle should replace the question mark?

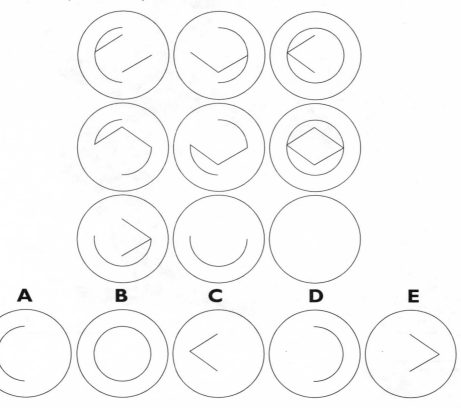

PUZZLE 81

Can you unravel the reasoning behind these diagrams and find the missing letter?

PUZZLE 82

Which number should replace the question mark?

PUZZLE 83

Which is the odd one out?

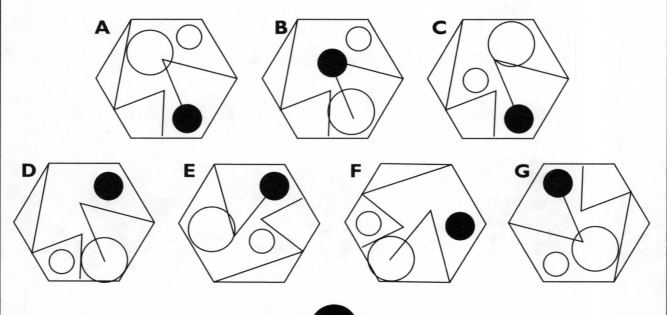

PUZZLE 84

Which is the odd one out?

13
20 29 7
17 49 136
19 115 23
40 52
319

PUZZLE 85

Each of the nine squares in the grid marked 1A to 3C should incorporate all the lines and symbols which are shown in the squares of the same letter and number immediately above and to the left. For example, 2B should incorporate all the lines and symbols that are in 2 and B.
One of the squares is incorrect. Which one is it?

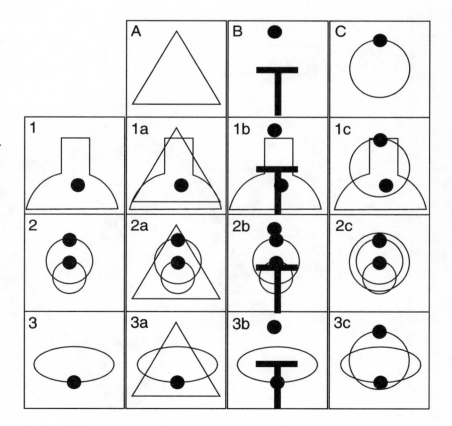

PUZZLE 86

There is an odd letter in each triangle, can you find them?

PUZZLE 87

Fill in the missing letter by following a definite rule.

PUZZLE 88

A man lived alone in a house for 3 months. He had no visitors and never left the house. One night he turned off the lights and left the house. He was never seen again. But his exit resulted in 100 people dying. **How was that?**

PUZZLE 89

A committee of 6 is to be formed from a group of seven men and four women. How many different committees can be formed if at least 2 women are included?

LEVEL 3

PUZZLE 90

At the local tennis club the following members entered the championships for singles and doubles:

	MEN	WOMEN
MENS SINGLES	40	
WOMENS SINGLES		30
MENS DOUBLES	20 pairs	
WOMENS DOUBLES		15 pairs
MIXED DOUBLES	30	30

It was a knockout contest so by using byes the numbers were reduced to 32-16-8-4-2

How many matches were played?

PUZZLE 91

What number should replace the question mark?

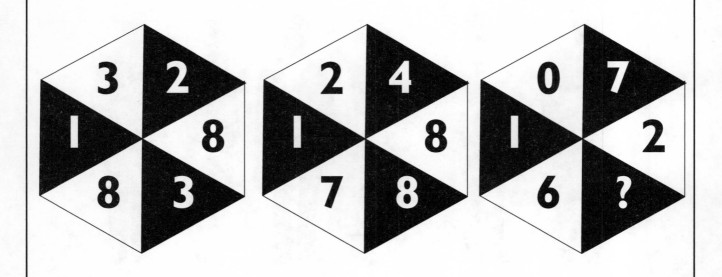

PUZZLE 92

Which word from the right-hand box continues the sequence in the left-hand box:

PIN

LIMIT

MILITIA

ALIBI

BIKINIS

SIEVE

VALID

REVERE

PUZZLE 93

What number should replace the question mark?

? 125

355 150

330 215

305 240

PUZZLE 94

Which is the odd figure out?

A

B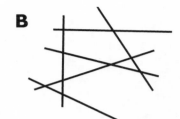

C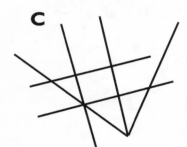

D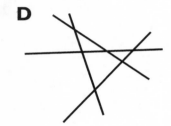

E

PUZZLE 95

Which word is the odd one out?

ODE	ICE	TOILED	ORDAIN
RADIAL	OAR	NEARER	CIRCLE
USE	AIL	OLD	POODLE
ACT	ERR	RAN	MOHAIR

PURSUE

PUZZLE 96

Arrange all of the letters of the newspaper headline below to spell out three animals.

HANGOVER KID BRA-STRAP PRANK

PUZZLE 97

The four pieces top, when fitted together correctly, form a circle. However, one has gone missing. Can you find which one it is?

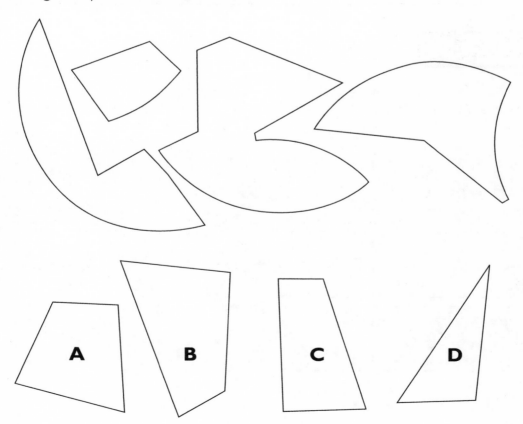

A   B   C   D

PUZZLE 98

What is the missing letter?

PUZZLE 99

Fill in the missing numbers; the link is the same in each line of numbers.

148	29	
	34	1849
925		

PUZZLE 100

What letter completes the pyramid?

PUZZLE 101

A fit young man died on a wide, flat grassy path 200 feet from a gate. Other than his clothes, all he had with him was a stick. He was not ill in any way, did not suffer a heart attack or stroke, and was not murdered or otherwise harmed by anyone.

How did he die?

PUZZLE 102

Which word is the odd one out?

ONE
LOG
TIE OAR
FEW HUE
MAT JAW
PEG

PUZZLE 103

The spine of this book contains the coded name of its author. Can you crack the code?

242 212 634 522 923 313 797 100 799

LEVEL 3

PUZZLE 104

What should appear in the square containing the question mark?

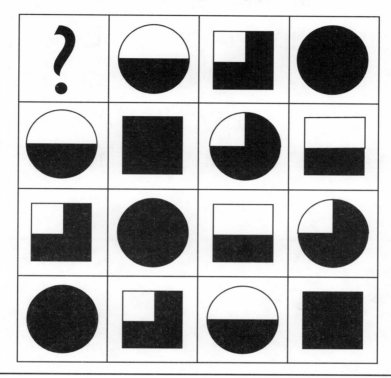

PUZZLE 105

Which word on the right should logically be transferred to join the list on the left?

AS
TO
OF
IN

DO
BE
IF
AM
IS

PUZZLE 106

A deaf, and blind man with no sense of smell is sitting in a room. Another person enters, carrying a closed cardboard box and sits down nearby. The first man quickly realizes that inside the box is a cat. **How?**

PUZZLE 107

How many lines appear in this figure?

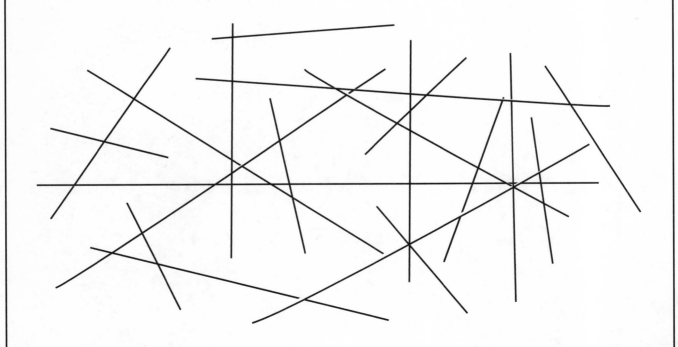

PUZZLE 108

What letter should replace the question mark?

L	E	I
?	E	N
T	H	F
T	E	T
C	R	R

PUZZLE 109

What word is indicated travelling round the circle in a clockwise direction?

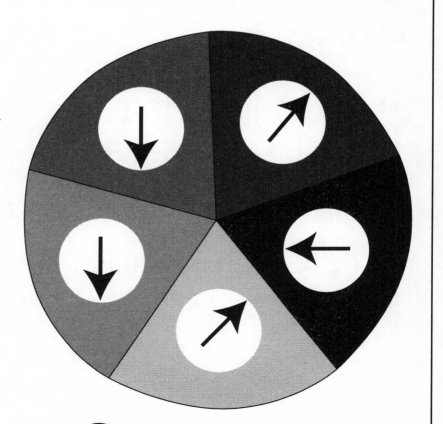

PUZZLE 110

What letters should replace the question marks?

PUZZLE 111

A man lies dead in a puddle of blood and water in a locked room. The coroner records a verdict of suicide.

Why?

PUZZLE 112

What letters should replace the question mark?

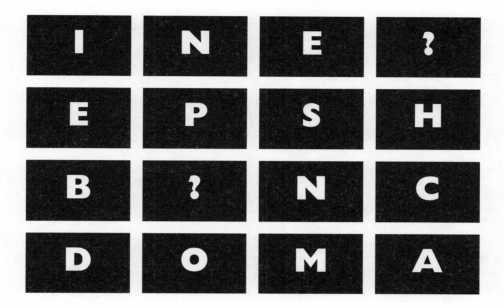

PUZZLE 113

What letter should replace the question mark?

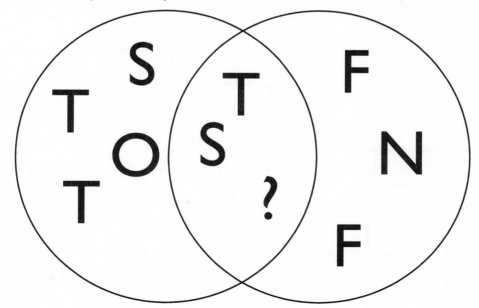

PUZZLE 114

Which is the missing tile?

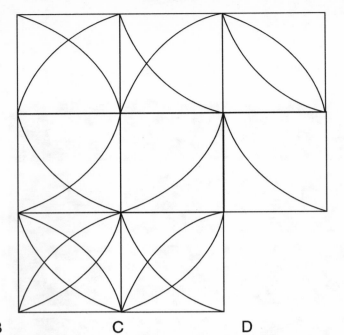

A   B   C   D   E

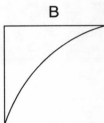 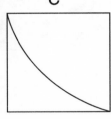 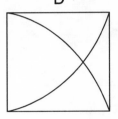 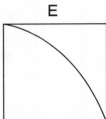

PUZZLE 115

What number should replace the question mark?

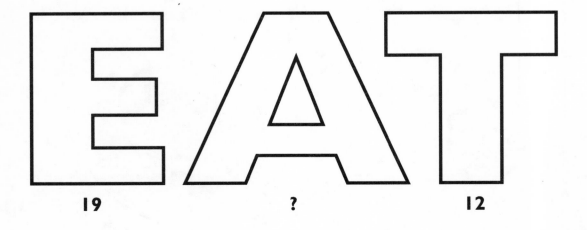

19   ?   12

LEVEL 3

PUZZLE 116

What letter should replace the question mark?

Y	S	T
N	A	?

O	A	A
A	H	I

U	Y	G
C	T	A

PUZZLE 117

Take one letter from each cloud in turn to spell out five astronomical words. Eight letters are left over which can be arranged to spell another astrological word.

1. G M C
   P U A

2. Q E E
   D N A

3. N N O
   U R I

4. I V L
   A U Y

5. M M R
   D E A

6. I R E
   I Z B

7. I R D
   U A S

8. S A E
   E N A

263

PUZZLE 117

How many times do the 10 letters 'QWERTYUIOP' appear in a straight line in any order. All 10 letters must be uninterrupted by other letters. They can appear horizontally, vertically, diagonally, backwards or forwards.

```
P S Q T R Y E W U P O Q I C D
O V Q W T W M Q O T K W L S W
I X P Q E P O I U Y T E W R Q
Y V O U C T U A V D B R N H O
U Y I W X Y R K R P E T Y O P
R P W E T B M Y P B J Y V I E
T Q U R E A E R U U F U C U I
W O E T Z J G Z F I W I P P R
E W Y Y N P Q C F C O O M Y U
Q E R I R T E Y U W I P O Q T
U R T O Q P I W T Y U E R T Y
J T A P Q O W E R T I Y U R E
S Y R C Q I U O P Y T W Q E R
P I O P U Q W E Y T R X V W K
J U D X D V B D S L K J Z K N
```

PUZZLE 119

The numbers 4, 2, 1, 9, 6, 3, are inserted in the grid to a certain pattern. Can you work out the pattern and complete the missing numbers?

4	3	6	9	1	2	4	3	6
2	1	9	6	3	4	2	1	9
1	2	4	3	6	9	1	2	4
9	4				1	9	6	3
6	3				2	4	3	6
3	6				4	2	1	9
4	9	6	9	6	3	4	3	6
2	1	3	1	3	6	2	1	9
1	2	4	2	4	9	1	2	4

PUZZLE 120

Where should the missing hour and on the fourth clock point to?

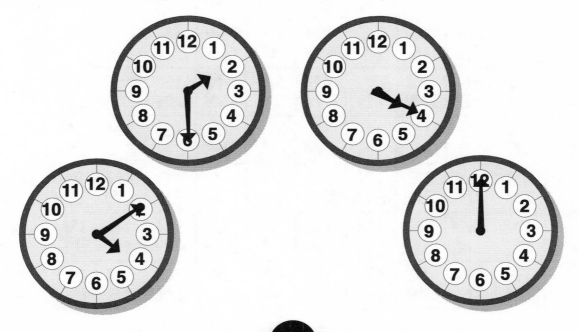

PUZZLE 121

A man is born in 1982 and dies in 1962 aged 35.
How is this possible?

PUZZLE 122

The diagram represents a treasure map. You must find the starting point and finish on the square marked T.

1S 2E means 1 South, 2 East.

Just one problem, you may have been sent on a wild goose chase as some squares are not used. If you cross out these squares a letter is revealed which may be the real source of the treasure. Can you find the hidden letter?

1E 3S	1E 2S	2S 2E	1S 2W	2E 4S	2E 2S	1W 1S	5S 2E	1E 3S	2S 3W
2S 3E	2S 1E	2E 4S	1E 2S	1N 2E	1N 1W	1W 5S	1S 2W	1E 1S	1W 1S
2N 2E	2N 2E	2W 3S	2E 2N	1N 4W	1N 2W	1W 2S	3S 2W	2N 1E	1W 4S
1E 3N	3S 1E	3N 2W	1W 2N	4S 2W	3N 2E	1N 3W	1E 3N	**T**	2S 2W
2S 4E	1E 1S	1S 1E	1S 1N	3S 1W	3N 1W	1N 2E	1E 3N	3N 1E	3N 3W
5E 2N	1W 3N	1E 2S	1N 1W	1N 3W	1N 4W	1W 2S	1E 2S	4N 1W	2S 2W
4N 1E	1W 2N	3N 5E	2N 1W	1S 4W	1S 4W	1S 2W	3N 1W	1S 1E	3W 1S
1E 2N	1W 4N	4E 2N	1N 3W	1N 3W	1N 4E	2E 3N	1W 1N	3N 1E	2N 1W

PUZZLE 123

What is the missing number?

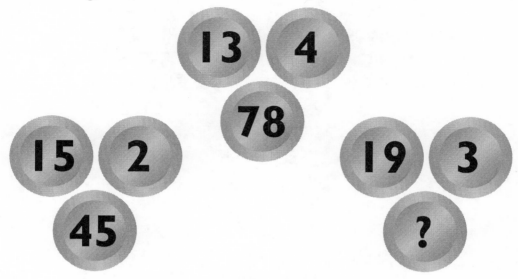

PUZZLE 124

Work out the reasoning behind the circles in this grid and fill in the square with the question mark.

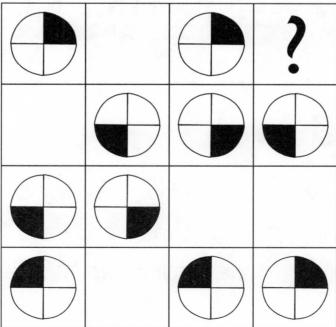

PUZZLE 125

Which of the following is not an anagram of 'SISTER SUSIE'S SEWING SHIRTS'?

THIS ISSUES WIRING STRESSES.
WRIGHTS ISSUES SENSITISERS.
SURE IS WISE STRESS INSIGHTS.
INSISTS WISH RISES GESTURES.
WISHES GESTURES SIR INSISTS.
STIRRING ISSUES SETS WISHES.
WIRES ISSUES THIS STRESSING.
STRESSES ISSUES IS WRITHING.
WITNESS RISES RIGHTS ISSUES.
ISSUES WRITES RESTS HISSING.
RIGHTS ISSUES WINS STRESSES.
WISHES TISSUES STIRS SINGER.
SURE SIGNS RISES IS THIS WEST.
STIRS WISHES RESISTS GENIUS.
INSISTS ISSUES REGRETS WISH.
ISSUES WITH RISING STRESSES.
ISSUES TIGERISHNESS WRISTS.
THESIS WRITERS ISSUES SIGNS.

PUZZLE 126

Whenever I warm a cup of milk for breakfast, I put one cup of milk in the microwave (which is in perfect working order) for exactly 75 seconds. **Why?**

PUZZLE 127

What shape is missing from the bottom section?

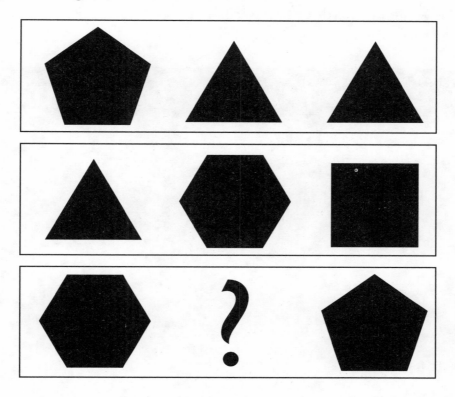

PUZZLE 128

What number should replace the question mark?

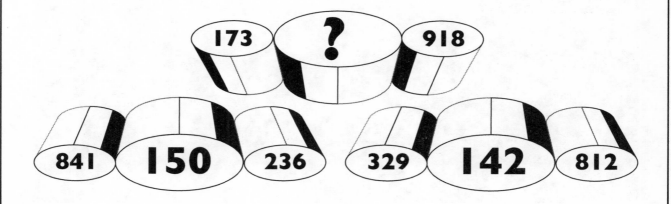

PUZZLE 129

In this grid the word 'POTATO', written without a change of direction, appears only once. It can be written forwards or backwards in a horizontal, vertical or diagonal direction. Can you spot it?

```
T O P P O T A T T O T P O P O
O O A A T O P A T O T A O P O T
P A P O T T P O T A T T O O A
T A P T O T O T O P O O A T T
O T O P A O T P P T P T P O A
O P A T O P A O A O T A T A P
A P O A P O T P T P T A T P T
T P A P A A P T O P T T O T A
O O O A T T A A O O P T A A T
T T O O A O T T O P O T A P O
O A T P T P T P A O T O T A P
P O O T A A P A T T O A A P O
P T A T T T T P O P O T T T T
O T A O O P T O P A T P O O O
O P P O T A T T A P A T P E P
```

PUZZLE 130

Working counter clockwise take one letter from each circle in turn to spell out three US cities. One word of warning, each of the names starts in a different circle.

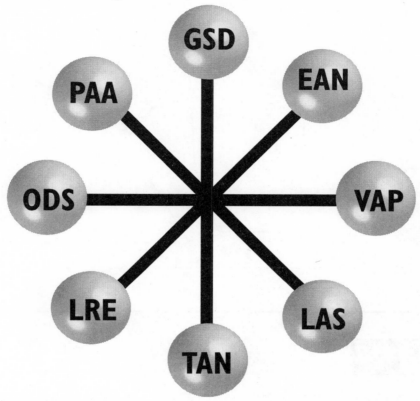

PUZZLE 131

Which girl on the right is able to complete the sequence on the left?

GAZEBO
ACCEDE
VERIFY

EUNICE
AGATHA
JOANNE
INGRID

PUZZLE 132

Arrange these pieces to construct a six-pointed star.

PUZZLE 133

To which of the boxes on the right can a dot be added so that both dots meet the same conditions as the box below?

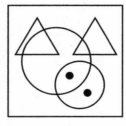

A   **B**   **C**   **D**   **E**

 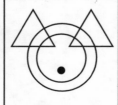   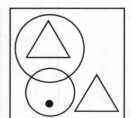

PUZZLE 134

A married couple go to a movie. During the main film the husband strangles his wife. He is able to get her body home without attracting attention. **How?**

PUZZLE 135

In how many ways can the word 'SURF' be read? Start at the central letter 'S' and surf your way to an adjoining letter up, down, backward or forward, in and out in any direction.

```
                    F
          F         R         F
      F   R         U         R   F
  F   R   U         S         U   R   F
      F   R         U         R   F
          F         R         F
                    U
                    R
                    F
```

LEVEL 3

PUZZLE 136

Each line and symbol which appears in the four outer circles is transferred to the center circle according to these rules:

If a line or symbol occurs in the outer circles:

Once:	it is transferrred
Twice:	it is possibly transferred
3 Times:	it is transferred
4 Times:	it is not transferred

Which of the circles A, B, C, D or E should appear at the center of the diagram?

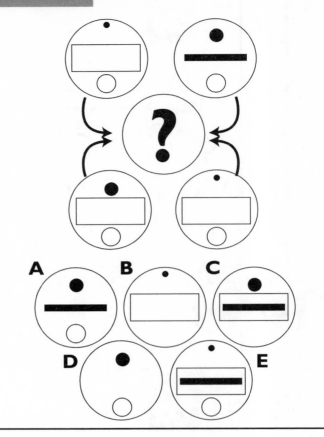

PUZZLE 137

Can your find the weight of each bag of corn?

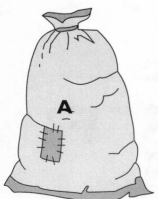 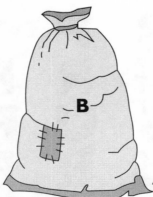 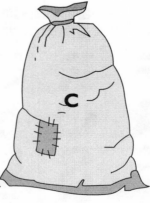 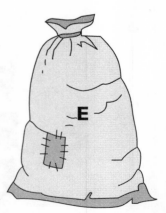

WT. 56lbs plus half its own weight

WT 54lbs plus one third of its own weight

WT 60lbs plus one quarter of its own weight

WT 64lbs plus one fifth of its own weight.

274

PUZZLE 138

Each of the nine squares in the grid marked 1A to 3C, should incorporate all the lines and symbols which are shown in the squares of the same letter and number immediately above and to the left. For example, 2B should incorporate all the lines and symbols that are in 2 and B. One of the squares is incorrect. Which one is it?

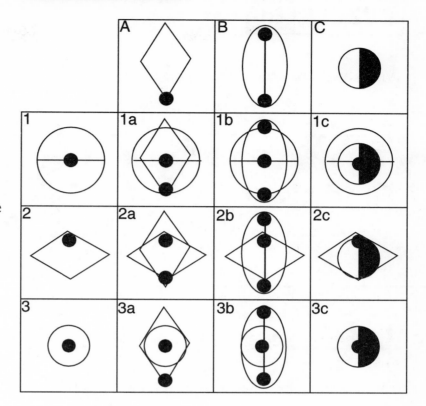

PUZZLE 139

Take a letter from each cloud in turn to find 6 six-letter terms associated with weather.

1. S B F Z N V
2. L R O U I E
3. L R M O I P
4. O H T G B T
5. E Y R U D H
6. Y X R S S T

PUZZLE 140

Which hexagon is the odd one out?

PUZZLE 141

Which of the following cubes cannot be made from this pattern?

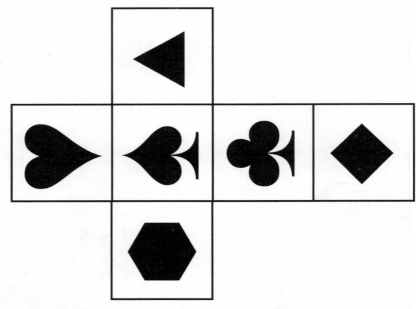

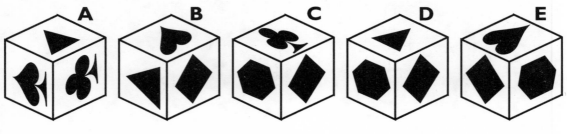

PUZZLE 142

Which is the odd one out?

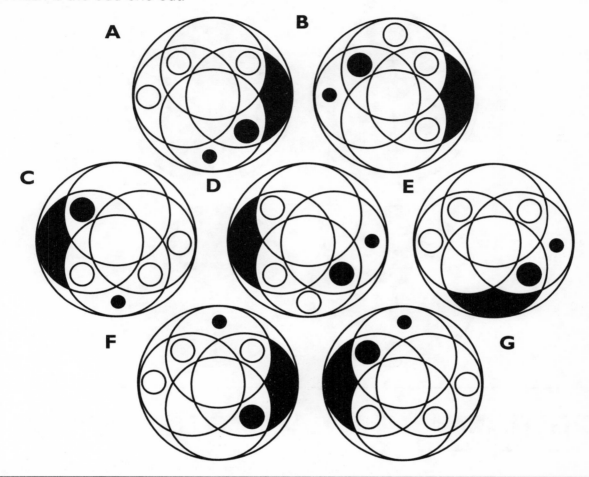

PUZZLE 143

Which word should be placed in the rectangle marked with a question mark?

ROCKET	EYELID	CRUISE
TATTOO	ANCHOR	NOZZLE
GRAVEL	LADDER	?

GUTTER
ESCUDO
POTEEN
SALVOS
QUOITS
RADISH

PUZZLE 144

Which letters should replace the question marks for a definite rule?

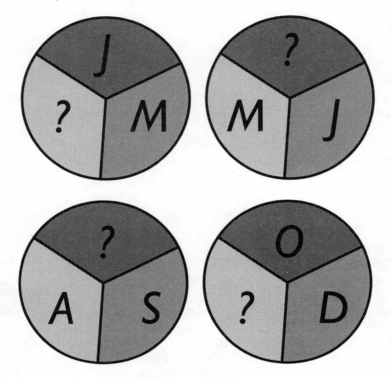

PUZZLE 145

Find the missing number.

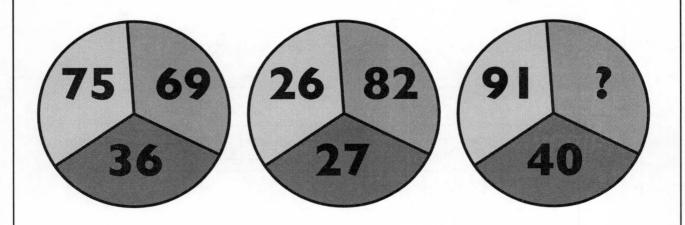

PUZZLE 146

Each pair of circles produces the circle above by carrying forward only those elements that are different. Similar elements are cancelled out.
Find the circle to replace the question mark.

A   **B**   **C**   **D**   **E**

PUZZLE 147

Fill in the missing number.

A	B	C
221	2211	2221
311	1321	11131211
131	111311	?

PUZZLE 148

These are anagrams of animals. What are they?

SOMEDAY   ORCHESTRA
DOING   TREES
CORONA   ALPINES

PUZZLE 149

Which hexagon is the odd one out?

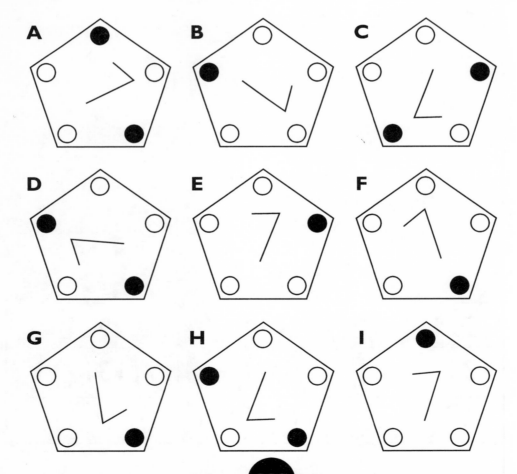

PUZZLE 150

Which is the odd word out?

KNOWLEDGE   SCENERY
TWOFOLD   AEON
LESSEE   DEBTOR

PUZZLE 151

How many triangles are there in this figure?

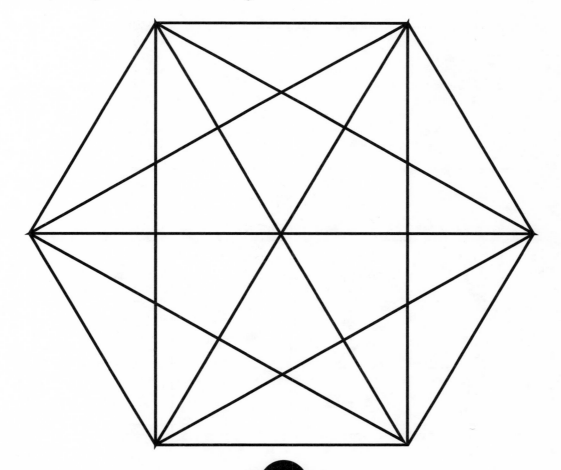

PUZZLE 152

Which pair of letters should replace the question mark?

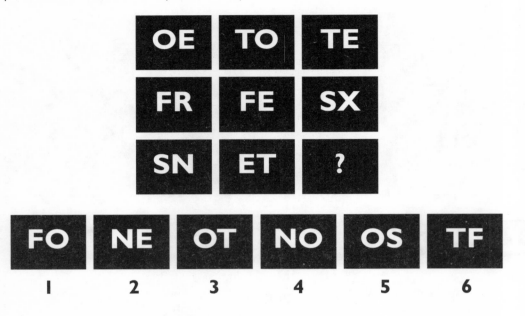

FO	NE	OT	NO	OS	TF
1	2	3	4	5	6

PUZZLE 153

Work out the pattern of the route and fnd out what should replace the question mark.

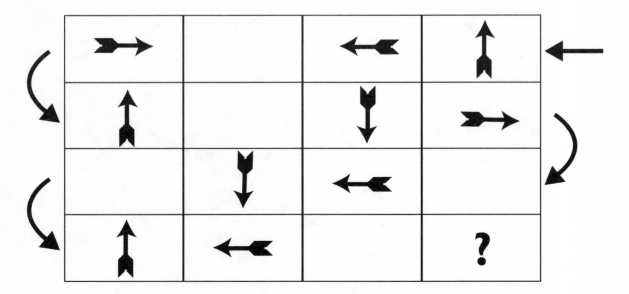

PUZZLE 154

Each line and symbol which appears in the four outer circles is transferred to the center circle according to these rules:
If a line or symbol occurs in the outer circles:

Once:	it is transferred
Twice:	it is possibly transferred
3 Times:	it is transferred
4 Times:	it is not transferred.

Which of the circles A, B, C, D or E should appear at the center of the diagram?

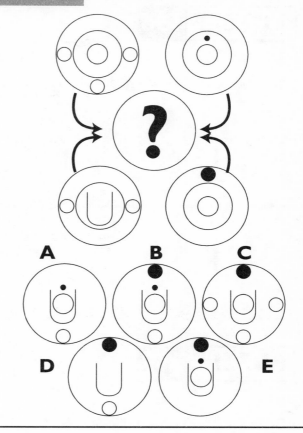

PUZZLE 155

This is an anagram of a fish.

We have given you the letters that you do not need. Find the missing letters, change their order, and you will find a fish

T D O X U Q E B N
Z L G P V J M K Y

PUZZLE 156

What number should replace the question mark?

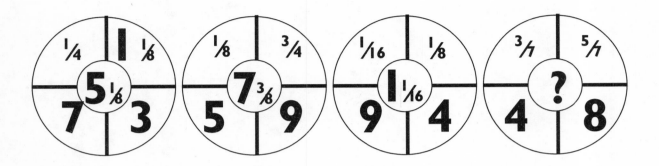

PUZZLE 157

There are 17 creatures hidden. How many creatures can you find in the square. You may move up or down, backwards or forward or diagonally but only in a straight line. Only 1 letter is not used.

K	R	A	V	D	R	A	A
A	A	T	L	Y	R	O	L
B	C	W	I	C	R	C	B
A	O	E	A	O	E	H	A
L	N	N	T	O	D	O	C
O	N	M	G	T	N	U	O
N	Y	A	A	O	A	G	R
E	E	A	R	W	I	G	H
			W		G	H	E

PUZZLE 158

Which hexagon below carries on the sequence A, B, C or D?

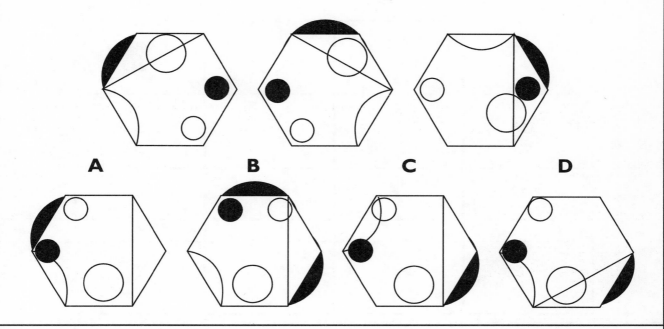

A   **B**   **C**   **D**

PUZZLE 159

Spell out a 10-letter word by moving into each circle once only.
Clue: a vegetable

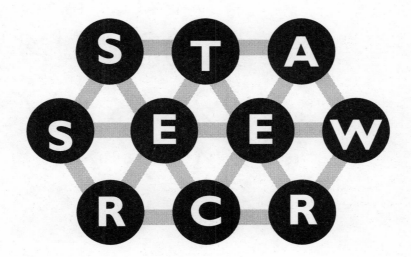

PUZZLE 160

Unravel the logic behind this diagram and find which symbol should go into the square marked ?

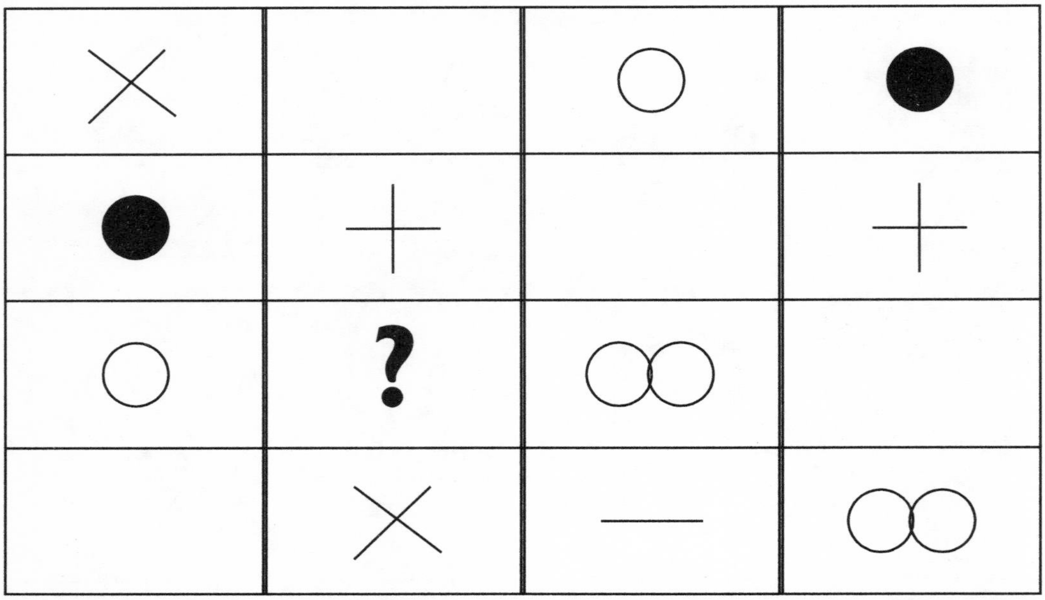

✕		○	●
●	+		+
○	?	∞	
	✕	—	∞

PUZZLE 161

Which is the odd one out?

6366   4328
5408   7142
7284   9273
5449   4328

PUZZLE 162

Multiply all the numbers from -10 to +10 in increments of one inclusive.

What is the result?

-10 x -9 x -8 x -7 x -6 ... +6 x +7 x +8 x +9 x +10

PUZZLE 163

Can you find the number that should replace the question mark?

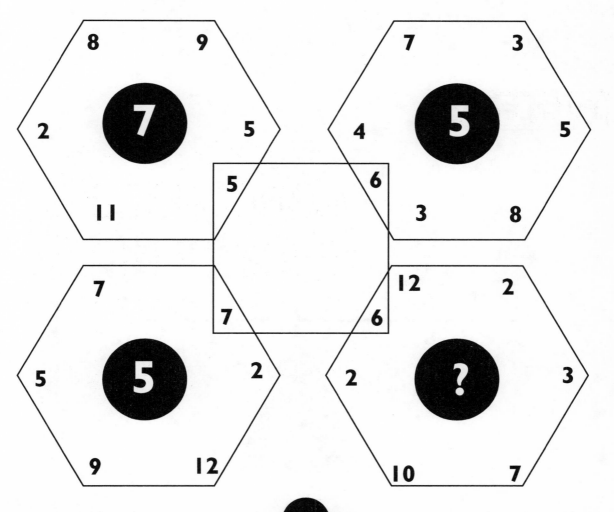

PUZZLE 164

Can you find the odd one out?

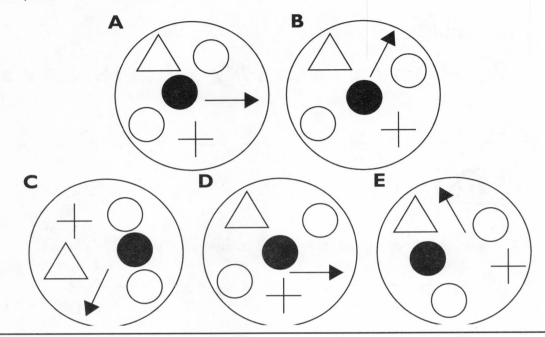

A   B   C   D   E

PUZZLE 165

What value weight should be placed at D to balance the scale?

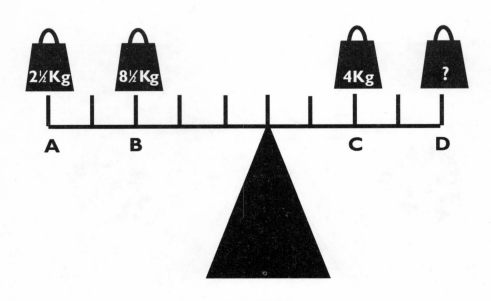

PUZZLE 166

Take one letter from each hexagon in turn and find six 6-letter vegetables.

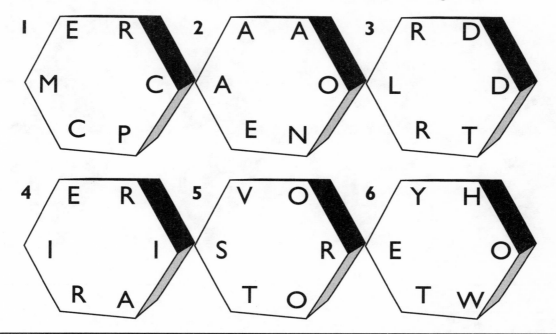

PUZZLE 167

Which pentagon completes the series A, B, C or D?

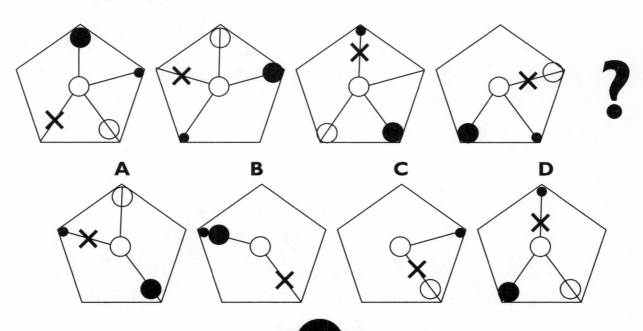

A   B   C   D

PUZZLE 168

Can you unravel the reasoning behind these diagrams and find the missing letter?

PUZZLE 169

The nicknames for these states have been mixed up. Can you sort them out?

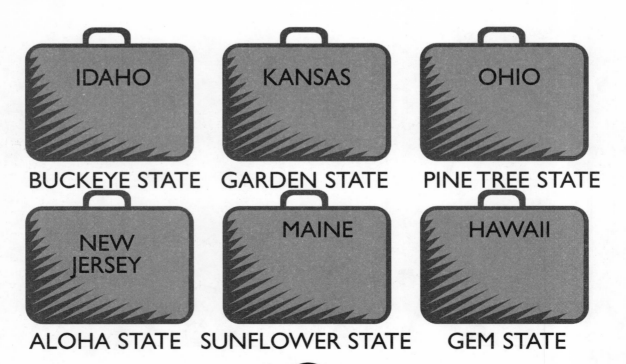

IDAHO

KANSAS

OHIO

BUCKEYE STATE   GARDEN STATE   PINE TREE STATE

NEW JERSEY

MAINE

HAWAII

ALOHA STATE   SUNFLOWER STATE   GEM STATE

PUZZLE 170

Each of the nine squares in the grid marked 1A to 3C, should incorporate all the lines and symbols which are shown in the squares of the same letter and number immediately above and to the left. For example, 2B should incorporate all the lines and symbols that are in 2 and B. One of the squares is incorrect. Which one is it?

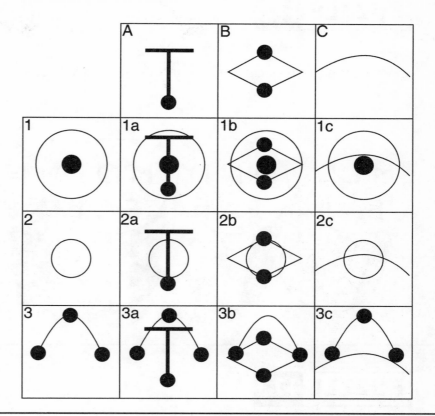

PUZZLE 171

What should the next fish look like?

PUZZLE 172

Which circle's letters cannot be rearranged into a 6-letter word.

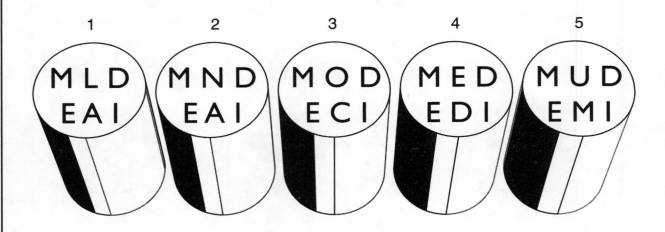

1	2	3	4	5
M L D	M N D	M O D	M E D	M U D
E A I	E A I	E C I	E D I	E M I

PUZZLE 173

Which is the odd one out?

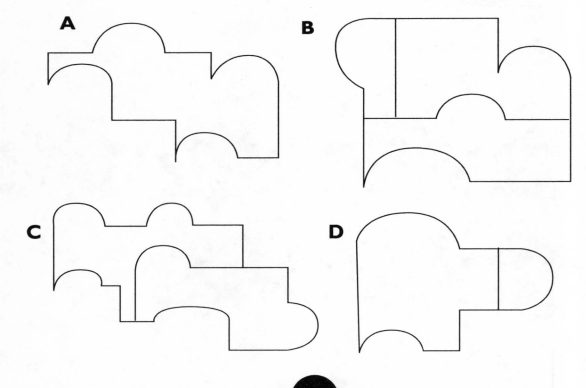

A   B   C   D

PUZZLE 174

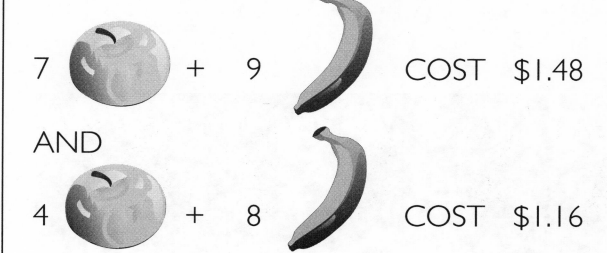

7 🍎 + 9 🍌 COST $1.48

AND

4 🍎 + 8 🍌 COST $1.16

HOW MUCH DOES I BANANA COST?

PUZZLE 175

Which is the odd one out?

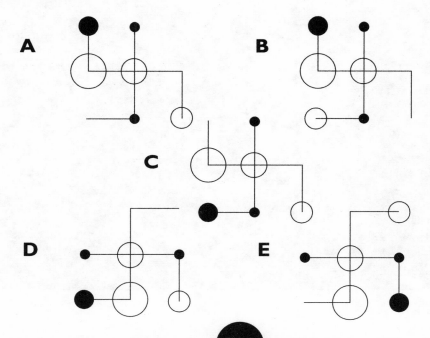

PUZZLE 176

There are 13 islands hidden in this square. How many islands can you find? You can move up or down, backwards and forward and diagonally but only in a straight line. Two letters are not used.

```
C A N A R I E S
I A T I T Y P O
R Y R A J L I L
A A L O I I A O
E N Y L L W F M
L O N G I I A O
A I K O O C N N
B A H A M A S E
```

PUZZLE 177

Which of these is not an anagram of mathematical terms?

L A C E S E N
B O S H R M U
N O G A T C O
L O C I D C Y
X H T R N A A

PUZZLE 178

Which temperature Celsius is the same as Fahrenheit?

PUZZLE 179

What is the answer to this sum?

$$7+6\times5-4\times8+17= \ ?$$

PUZZLE 180

Find pairs of letters to form four 4-letter birds, one pair is not used.

DO	AK	GU
LL	OW	TE
KI	DO	CR

1. Starting with 'A' move 5 letters forward in the alphabet, then 2 letters back.

2. C.
The shaded portions indicate calculations by 0.5 and 0.75.
244 × 0.75 = 183
264 × 0.5 = 132
Similarly
584 × 0.75 = 438
374 × 0.5 = 187

3. T
To obtain the letter in the overlapping portion take the alphabetical values of the consonants only. Add the value and take the corresponding value letter of the alphabet.
Thus M (13) + D (4) + C (3) = 20
T is the twentieth letter of the alphabet.

4. 1121
Add up the first digits of all the other numbers to obtain 11, then add up the second digits to obtain 21.

5.

Start at the top left-hand square and move along the top row and back along the bottom row. The circle moves one corner clockwise at each stage alternating black and white.

6.

Looking across, the third box is a combination of the three other boxes in the same line, except when the three boxes contain a line more than once in the same position it is cancelled out.

7. E
Read along the top letters of the pyramid first, then along the bottom letters to spell out the phrase "ERROR MESSAGE".

8. ELECTRIC LAMP
THOMAS ALVA EDISON

9. 18
In the odd numbered segments add the two numbers on the outside together and multiply by 2 to obtain the number in the center in the segment opposite. In the even numbered segments add the outside numbers and divide by 2 to obtain the number opposite.

10. T
Taking their respective positions in the alphabet opposite letter values add up to 20. The twentieth letter in the alphabet is T. The same system applies to the other two stars.

11. B.
It is the only one which is not a mirror image of its neighbor looking across and down.

12. 12
Divide the top left-hand number by 3. Divide the top right-hand number by 4. Then multiply the two results together to arrive at the bottom number.

13. The sequence runs:

Start at the bottom left-hand square and move up the column then down the next etc.

14. TY
Read across identical sections in each square to spell out four 8-letter words
A=MACARONI
B=DECIMATE
C=APPRAISE
D=TENACITY

15.

Every fourth box is the result of combining the contents of the three previous boxes, except where a line appears in the same position more than once it is not carried forward.

16. CORIOLANUS was written by Shakespeare.
BARNABY RUDGE
OLIVER TWIST
EDWIN DROOD
were all written by Charles Dickens.

17. 66
Take every possible combination of the circled digits and divide by 9

459	9	=	51
495	9	=	55
549	9	=	61
594	9	=	66
945	9	=	105
954	9	=	106

18. Number 5
In the top left-hand corner segment of the grid.

19. D.
Each horizontal line contains a curved line, a figure with straight lines only, a closed symmetrical figure and a closed asymmetrical figure.

20.
ERMINE
DEXTER
ARGENT
HELMET
CHARGE
MULLET (scrambled)

21. 8
The right-hand circle contains the sum of all the two figure combinations of the three-figure number 964. The left-hand circle contains the same for 835.

835:			
	8+3	=	11
	8+5	=	13
	3+5	=	8

22. C.
The figure at the top increases its number of sides by two and moves to the right. The figure at the bottom increases its number of sides by one and moves to the left.

23. 19
The left circle contains the sums of the digits of the four-figure numbers in the right circle and the right circle vice versa.

24. D.

25. B.

26. Looking across the contents of alternate boxes are a mirror image.

27. J
Each number represents its position in the grid i.e. 13 is in Row 1, Column 3. Place 21, therefore, on Row 2, Column 1. Add the digits of each number and count the same number of spaces along one row and back along the next row to place the appropriate numbered letter of the alphabet.

28. 129
All other numbers have an anagram pairing i.e. a number which uses the same three digits.

29.
E   H   K   N
Each grid works anti-clockwise starting at the top and finishing in the middle square. The first grid starts 'A' and jumps one letter at a time, the second starts 'B' jumping two at a time, the third 'C' jumping three and the fourth jumping four.

30. C.
In all the others there are twice as many straight lines as curved lines.

31. The letter E appears on its side in the middle of the square.

32. The five symbols appear in the following order.

Start at the top right-hand corner and work down the first column and up the second etc.

33. The letter A
The remaining letters can be arranged to spell 'ISOSCELES'

34. 15
There are four progressions of numbers from first to last pentagon.
1, 7, 13, 19, (add 6)
2, 5, 8, 11, (add 3)
2, 4, 6, 8, (add 2)
5, 9, 13, 17, (add 4)

35. RACE = 7
Deduct the number of curved lines from the number of straight lines in each word i.e. RACE has 9 straight lines and 2 curved lines.

36.

37. A.
The contents of each pentagon is determined by the contents of the two pentagons below it. Any lines which appear in both pentagons disappear. Only lines which appear in one pentagon only are carried forward.

38. GONE WITH THE WIND – MARGARET MITCHELL

39. A.
The value of the white dot = 2
The value of the black dot = 1
The total values within the hexagons = 1,2,3,4,5 and 6.

40. 36. Add the three numbers in the corner of each square, then add the digits of the same numbers and deduct to arrive at the number in the overlapping corner.
12+14+26= 52

1+2+1+ 4+2+6= 16
52-16= 36

41.

27	41	15	32	39	61	4	30
44	28	T	56	12	31	60	62
42	63	40	16	3	21	33	11
14	57	26	5	29	2	38	47
25	59	13	54	22	34	10	20
58	6	43	1	46	50	48	52
17	55	45	35	8	23	19	37
53	24	7	18	49	36	51	9

42.
AMUNDSEN
COLUMBUS
MAGELLAN

43. REMAIN:
All other words contain an internal rhyme – WAY-LAY DIS-MISS FUR-THER BACK-PACK.

44.
L   K   L
K   K   K
K   Y   K
The sequence runs XYPTTZYKKL. Start at the top right-hand corner and work around the perimeter spiralling inwards to finish in the centre.

45. C.
'A' is the same as 'D' with black/white reversal. 'B' is the same as 'E' with black/white reversal.

46. E.

47.

Start at bottom left-hand square and spiral in to the center in this order:
and then repeat.

48. C.
Each bottom pair of circles are added to produce the circle above, but like symbols disappear

49. SPRINGFIELD
Each car's destination began with the last letter of its starting place.
OAKLAND - DENVER etc.

298

50.
Turn 180° clockwise, miss 1 square, turn anticlockwise and repeat.

51.

52. GERFALCON

53. 1 ¾
1 ¾=(18 x⅙) -(5x¼)

54. E.
Startiing at the bottom circle combine elements with adjacent circles,but eliminating repeated elements, to form third circles. Then again from third circles to make topmost.

55.
CENTAVO
GUILDER
PIASTRE
DENARII
MILREID (not an anagram)

56. 4
1.   SCRIPT
2.   CRISPS
3.   CRISIS
4.   CANNOT BE ARRANGED
5.   DISCUS

57. WINDJAMMER

58. C.

59. He was lying outside a jeweller's shop with a brick by his side.
He had tried to break the window with a brick but the brick had rebounded and knocked him out.

60. D.
A. is the same as G.
F. is the same as E.
B. is the same as C.

61. Square should be blank
Start from the bottom right corner, move round counterclockwise in a spiral following the sequence.

1.   2.   3.   4.
●   ●   Blank   ○
         ○

62. The man had return tickets but his wife only had a single.

63. WHITING
Initial letters also spell a fish
WRASSE

64. The outer digits and up to the central digit except for 471.

65. Take the hour hand away from the minute hand to give the hour hand on the next clock.
Clock   1   6-2=   4
         2   11-4=   7
         3   7-4=   3
         4   9-3=   6
         5 HOUR HAND = 6
For the minute hand add 5 each time
Clock   1   6
         2   6+5=   11
         3   11+5=   4
         4   4+5=   9
         5   9+5=   2

66. A.

67. 48
Take a third of the number on the top left. Double the number on the top right. Multiply the two answers and place the product in the bottom circle.

68. 10
(A) Add the 4 numbers on the inside of the 4 pentagons.
(B) Add the digits of each sum.
Divide (A) by (B) and place in the corner of the square.

69. C.
Arrow points between
    △ and   ○
but C. the arrow points between
    △ and   ●

70. The authorities would have tampered with one parachute, but requesting two, they would have thought he could be taking a hostage.

71. 27
Each number represents the number of spaces between letters multiplied by 3.
O-T   4x3
T-K   8x3
K-A   9x3
A-H   6x3
H-O   6x3

72. 10
Multiply the two outside numbers together in each segment and alternately divide the product by 5 and then 6, and place the answer in the center of the opposite segment.

73. 6KG
L.H.
A   2x10=   20
B   5x5=   25
                    45
R.H.
C   3x5=   15
D   5x6=   30
                    45

74. He had ordered a bicycle which had arrived in 185 pieces for assembly, which was not stated in the catalogue, so this was his revenge.

75.
BARBEL
BURBOT
DUGONG
GROUPER
CUCKOO   (= bird)
MINNOW

76. D.

77.
BABOON
COUGAR
HEIFER
JAGUAR
POSSUM

78.

K	=	4
N	=	6
M	=	2
L	=	8

79. D.

○ moves 90° clockwise each step

● moves 180° each step

➤ moves 90° anti-clockwise each step

✗ moves 180° each step

80. E.

First two figures in each row are added together to form the third, but like elements cancel out.

81. Y

Spells TRIANGULARLY

82. 43

They are a series of prime numbers 29-31-37-41

83. B.

A. is the same as G.

C. is the same as E.

D is the same as F.

84. 19

Each number has a partner except 19. i.e.

23x5(ADD DIGITS)=	115
17x8(ADD DIGITS)=	136
20x2(ADD DIGITS)=	40
13x4(ADD DIGITS)=	52
29x11(ADD DIGITS)=	319
7x7(ADD DIGITS) =	49

85. 2C • missing at top of circle.

86. Triangle 1:   H

Only letter made up of only straight lines.

Triangle 2:   O

Only letter not made up of only straight lines.

87. O

O is the same number of spaces

from	F+X	9 spaces
	I+U	6 spaces
	L+R	3 spaces

88. He was a lighthouse keeper. His actions caused a ship-wreck which caused the death of 100 people.

89. 371

Assume 2 women and 4 men

Then

$\frac{4 \times 3}{2 \times 1}$ $\frac{7 \times 6 \times 5 \times 4}{4 \times 3 \times 2 \times 1} = 6 \times 35 = 210$

Assume 3 women and 3 men

Then

$\frac{4 \times 3 \times 2}{3 \times 2 \times 1}$ $\frac{7 \times 6 \times 5}{3 \times 2 \times 1} = 4 \times 35 = 140$

Assume 4 women and 2 men

Then

$\frac{4 \times 3 \times 2 \times 1}{4 \times 3 \times 2 \times 1}$ $\frac{7 \times 6}{2 \times 1} = 1 \times 21 = 21$

                                        371

90. 130

As there was only 1 winner (or in doubles a pair of winners) from each match, the matches played were as follows:

	MEN	WOMEN	LOSERS	WINNERS
MENS SINGLES	40	-	39	1
WOMENS SINGLES	-	30	29	1
MENS DOUBLES	20 pairs	-	19 pairs	1 pair
WOMENS DOUBLES	-	15 pairs	14 pairs	1 pair
MIXED DOUBLES	30	30	29 pairs	1 pair

130 MATCHES

91. 7

The number formed at the top of the hexagon is the bottom 2 digits multiplied by 16.

$67 \times 16 = 1072$

92. SIEVE

Delete alternate letters to reveal the Roman numeral sequence;

I, II, III, IV.

93. 420

They are times without the punctuation, with 25 minutes added each time:

1.25, 1.50, 2.15, 2.40, 3.05, 3.30, 3.55, 4.20.

94. D.

All the other figures contain twice as many lines as triangles.

95. ACT

All other three-letter words are spelled out by alternate letters of the six-letter words:

ODE	POODLE
ICE	CIRCLE
OAR	MOHAIR
USE	PURSUE
AIL	RADIAL
OLD	TOILED
ERR	NEARER
RAN	ORDAIN

96. AARDVARK, SPRINGBOK, PANTHER.

97. B.

98. H.

Starting at the head and working clockwise the sequence of second letters in the numbers ONE, TWO, THREE, FOUR, FIVE appears.

99. These are backwards way numbers and squares:

$29^2 = 841$	$92^2 = 8464$
$34^2 = 1156$	$43^2 = 1849$
$23^2 = 529$	$32^2 = 1024$

148	29	8464
6511	34	1849
925	23	1024

100. A.

Taking their respective value in the alphabet each mini-group of three circles totals 20.

E.g.   J = 10   G = 7   C = 3

101. He was a jockey. The gate was the starting gate of a race. He falls off his horse shortly after the race starts and is killed. The stick is his riding crop.

102. PEG

Taking the value of their positions in the alphabet the 3 letters in all of the other words add up to 34.

103. Add the three digits of each number together and take the respective letters of the alphabet to spell out 'HEMINGWAY'.

104.

Start at the bottom left-hand square and move along the bottom then back along the next line etc.
The sequence runs circle/square/circle etc., and the shading is full, three-quarters, half irrespective of whether it is a circle or square.

105. BE
When the last letter is repeated it forms another word (BEE). As do: AS (ASS), TO (TOO), OF (OFF) and IN (INN).

106. He is allergic to cats and feels his allergy symptoms coming on.

107. 20

108. G.
Work to the pattern shown below to spell out 'LEFT RIGHT CENTER'.

1	11	6
7	2	12
13	8	3
4	14	9
10	5	15

109. NEWNESS

NE	↗
W	←
NE	↗
S	↓
S	↓

110. T in the left disc and V in the right.
If the alphabet were written in a circle working clockwise the letters in the left circle would immediately precede vowels; in the right circle they follow vowels.

111. He stabbed himself with an icicle.

112. R is missing from both squares to spell out DOBERMAN PINSCHER using the route shown below.

113. E (for Eight).
The letters in the left circle are initials of numbers 1 - 10 spelled with 3 letters.
The bottom circle are numbers spelled with 4 letters.
The overlapping section are numbers spelled with 5 letters.

114. E.
Looking both across and down any lines common to the first two squares are not carried forward to the third square.

115. 16
Imagine the alphabet written in a circle. Count back from the letter the number of sides: E in the drawing has 12 sides. Count backwards 12 places to S, which is letter number 19 in the alphabet.

116. N
Work down the top letters of the first column then back up the bottom letters, then do the same with columns 2 and 3 to spell out the phrase:
"YOU CAN SAY THAT AGAIN".

117.
AQUARIUS
GANYMEDE
UNIVERSE
MERIDIAN
PENUMBRA
ZODIACAL (Scrambled)

118.

119. Starting at the bottom right-hand square the pattern is as follows:

The missing numbers are:

2	4	2
1	3	1
9	6	9

120. It should point to 3.
The minute hand goes back two at every stage.
The position of the hour hand is determined by the two numbers which the hands point to on the previous clock face added together then divided by 2.

121. He is born in Room 1982 of a hospital and dies in hospital Room 1962.

122. Visit the squares in the following order:

15	28	43	12	73	4	71	32	19	67
45	13	47	57	70	72	24	55	50	65
42	11	29	3	44	56	68	5	66	51
27	16	14	46	58	31	2	18	T	20
38	7			69	74	49	64	23	
30	41	8		48	6	60	21	54	33
10	37	17		39	25	35	1	52	62
40	26	59	9	36	61	63	34	22	53

123. 85.5
Divide the top left number by 2, multiply the top right by 3 and multiply the results together to get the bottom number.
19 / 2 = 9.5
3 × 3 = 9
9 × 9.5 = 85.5

124. The sequence starts at the top left-hand corner and runs down the first column, then up the second etc. The pattern is miss 1 square, black moves 180°, turn 90° clockwise, then miss 1 square 180° etc.

125.
RIGHTS ISSUES WINS STRESSES

126
When I put the cup in the microwave the handle is pointing towards me. The microwave has a revolving plate. After 75 seconds the handle is again in its initial position and I can remove the cup without burning my hand.

127. Total number of sides increases by 2 on each line: 11, 13, 15.

128. 182. Add the number formed by digits in these positions:
1 7 3   9 1 8
A B C   D E F
AC+DE+ BF= 13 + 91 + 78 = 182

129.
```
T O P P O T A T T O T P O P O
O A A T O P A T O T A O P O T
P A P O T T P O T A T T O O A
T A P T O T O T O P O O A T T
O T O P A O T P P T P T P O A
O P A T O P A O A O T A T A P
A P O A P O T P T P T A T P T
T P A P A A P T O P T T O T A
O O O A T T A A O O P T A A T
T T O O A O T T O P O T A P O
O A T P T P T P A O T O T A P
P O O T A A P A T T O A A P O
P T A T T T T P O P O T T T T
O T A O O P T O P A T P O O O
O P P O T A T T A P A T P E P
```

130.
LAS VEGAS
PORTLAND
PASADENA

131. AGATHA
The words use the letters A to H in order in the same position.
GAZEBO
ACCEDE
VERIFY
AGATHA

132.

133. E.
So that one dot appears in the small circle only, and one dot appears in both the large and small circle.

134. The movie is in a drive-in theater.

135. 28

136. C.

137.
A	112 lbs
B	81 lbs
C	80 lbs
D	80 lbs

138. 1B

139.
ZEPHYR
VORTEX
SULTRY
NIMBUS
FLOODS
BRIGHT

140. Number 3
RHYME has a vowel, the others are consonants.
1.   CRYPT
2.   SYLPH
3.   TRYST
4.   THYMY

141. A

142. E.
A is the same as G
B is the same as D
C is the same as F

143. ESCUDO
Initial letters spell 'RECTANGLE'.

144. The letters are the initial letters of the 12 months of the year.
1. F
2. A
3. J
4. N

145. 69
The top left number is a quarter of the other two numbers added.

146. C.
The two lower circles are added to produce the circle above but similar symbols disappear.

147.
311321 (Three ones, one three and two ones)
Box B describes A read aloud
Box C describes B read aloud
i.e.
131 becomes one one (11), one three (13) and one one (11) or 111311.
1-1   = 11
  1-3   = 1113
     1-1 = 111311

148.
SAMOYED
DINGO
RACOON
CARTHORSE
STEER
SPANIEL

149. E.
A is the same as H
B is the same as F
C is the same as D
G is the same as J

150. LESSEE
All contain silent letters
KNOWLEDGE
TWOFOLD
SCENERY
AEON
DEBTOR

151. 110

152. Number 2 - NE
The letters are the first and last
letters of the numbers 1 to 9.

153.

Turn 90° anticlockwise, miss 1 square,
turn 180° anticlockwise.

154. B.

155. CRAWFISH

156. 7 ⅗
(4 × ⅗) + (8 × ⅝)

157.
AARDVARK
ALBACORE
ABALONE
EARWIG
WAGTAIL
GANDER
BONGO
COD
MOA
OWL
RAT
RAM
LORY
COOT
CHOUGH
RACOON
NEWT.

158. D.

159. WATERCRESS

160. Square should be –
Start from the top left-hand corner,
move round clockwise in a spiral
following the sequence.
X blank ○● + blank ○○ –

161. 5449. The outer two numbers
multiplied together equal the inner
two numbers except for 5449.

162. 0
You multiply X O eventually.

163. 6
Add the five numbers in the hexagon
and divide the total by the number in
the square.
12 + 2 + 3 + 7+ 10 + 2 = ³⁶⁄₆ = 6

164. E. In each figure except E the
dark circle lies between the two light
circles.

165. 6KG
L.H.
A 3 × 8 ½ =   25 ½
B 5 × 2 ½ =   12 ½
                 38
R. H.
C 2 × 4 =   8
D 5 × 6 =   30
                 38

166.
ENDIVE
CARROT
CELERY
RADISH
POTATO
MARROW

167. B.
○ moves 144° anticlockwise
• moves 144° clockwise
X moves 72° clockwise
● moves 72° clockwise

168. D.
Spells DIAMONDS

169.
1. IDAHO   GEM STATE
2. KANSAS   SUNFLOWER STATE
3. OHIO   BUCKEYE STATE
4. NEW JERSEY   GARDEN STATE
5. MAINE   PINE TREE STATE
6. HAWAII   ALOHA STATE

170. 3B

171. The eighth fish should look to
the left, have a row of four pits along
its midline, and no pair of lower fins.

172.
1.   MEDIAL
2.   MEDIAN
3.   MEDICO
4.   CANNOT BE ARRANGED
5.   MEDIUM

173. A.
A. has 4 curved lines and 9 straight
lines. The remainder has twice as
many straight lines as curved lines.

174. 1 banana costs 11 cents.
7A+9B   COST   1.48
4A+8B   COST   1.16
28A+36B COST   5.92
28A+56B COST   8.12

SUBTRACT 20B   COST   2.20
         1B   COST   11

175. A.
B is the same as D
C is the same as E

176.
BALEARIC
CANARIES
CAROLINE
BAHAMAS
SOLOMON
MALTA
TAIWAN
SCILLY
FIJI
COOK
LONG
IONA
EPI

177.
SCALENE
RHOMBUS
OCTAGON
CYCLOID
ANTHRAX (not an anagram of math-
ematical terms)

178. -40C Same as -40F
-40 C × ⅝ + 32 = -40F
or
-40F - 32 × ⅝ = -40C

179. Sums of this type must have the
following rules applied

Work out the different parts of the
calculation in the following order:
( ) bracketed pieces take top priority;
then come multiplications and
divisions; and addition and
subtraction take place last.
Therefore
7 + (6 × 5) - (4 × 8) + 17 =
7 + 30 - 32 + 17 = 22

180.
GULL
CROW
DODO
KITE